FORGOTTEN CIVILIZATIONS

The Rediscovery of India's Lost History

Rupa Gupta
and
Gautam Gupta

First published in India in 2021 by Hachette India
(Registered name: Hachette Book Publishing India Pvt. Ltd)
An Hachette UK company
www.hachetteindia.com

SRD

Cover illustration based on the lithograph 'Dusaswumedh Ghat. Benares,' by the Anglo-Indian scholar James Prinsep. Courtesy of the British Library, London.

ISBN 978-93-91028-47-3

Hachette Book Publishing India Pvt. Ltd
4th & 5th Floors, Corporate Centre,
Plot No. 94, Sector 44, Gurugram – 122003, India

Typeset in Bembo Std on 11.5/15.8
by Jojy Philip, New Delhi – 15

Printed and bound in India
by Manipal Technologies Limited, Manipal

This book is dedicated to
Wg. Cdr. A.K. Das Gupta

CONTENTS

INTRODUCTION

Lifting the Veil from India's Past

Our narrative begins in the early eighteenth century, a period when the Western world knew virtually nothing about India, and the little that was known was a distorted and exoticized idea of the Orient. The people of the subcontinent were perceived as barbaric and uncivilized – it seemed implausible that such a land could possess a history or culture worthy of any attention from the rest of the world. Imperialist condescension notwithstanding, one of the reasons for this perception was the lack of historical documentation in the modern sense. In the absence of written documentation about ancient India, it was believed that history in the subcontinent began only with the Mughals. Veritably, the general populace of the subcontinent knew practically nothing about their own cultural or historical inheritance.

A key reason for this was the fact that most Indians had no access to Sanskrit, one of the major languages along with Pali, in which ancient Indian wisdom was recorded. Sanskrit, considered the language of the gods, was jealously guarded by brahmin pandits who considered themselves the sole keepers of ancient wisdom. No other caste was allowed to learn the language, and it was considered a sin if they attempted to do so. In fact, they gatekept the language to such an extent that a well-known Scottish philosopher and mathematician of the time, Dugald Stewart (1753-1828), tried to prove in an essay that the Sanskrit language did not exist at all, and that it was a farce made up by the priestly class of India.

And yet, barely a century later, Mark Twain, the famed American author who visited India in 1896, went into raptures about the country, calling it 'the cradle of the human race, the birthplace of human speech, the mother of history... Our most valuable and most instructive materials in the history of man are treasured up in India only!' Quite a turnaround, indeed.

The credit for this extraordinary feat of recovering India's hidden centuries goes to a handful of Englishmen who had arrived in India in the eighteenth century. Their natural curiosity to discover the country's ancient cultural heritage, coupled with an academic discipline in recording their findings, allowed them to succeed in 'restoring India to her rightful place among the civilizations of the world.'[1] Some studied the ancient Sanskrit manuscripts to understand the unique cultural traditions. Others traversed the length and breadth of the country – travelling hundreds of miles on horseback, camels or elephants, studying ancient monuments. Yet others tried to prise open the locked doors of the past by deciphering inscriptions written in long-forgotten scripts.

---

1 David Kopf, *British Orientalism and the Bengal Renaissance: The Dynamics of Indian Modernization*, University of California Press, 1969.

In the process, and through their writings and publications, these men made vast and comprehensive contributions to Indic studies. They were responsible for popularizing oriental studies in Europe and for bringing about a huge change in the way India was perceived by the world. The stories we choose to explore in this book are of these ordinary English civil servants who managed to resurrect the knowledge of one of the greatest civilizations the world has ever known.

We shall trace the lives and times of 15 extraordinary scholars who voyaged across oceans and braved dense forests, displaying phenomenal courage and persistence in their zeal to discover India's history. Among these trailblazers were eminent orientalists such as William Jones, Charles Wilkins, Nathaniel Halhed, James Prinsep, H.T. Colebrooke, George Grierson and B.H. Hodgson. We shall see how, in the absence of written records or documentation, these pioneers found innovative ways to glean India's hidden past.

However, in writing this book, neither do we intend to hold a brief for the British colonial rule nor offer justification for the ruinous effects of their economic policies, their saga of exploitation, man-made famines, wars, racism, maladministration and more. Our narrative is not intended to be a defence of the British civilians who were perceived as alien freebooters either. Instead, it is an attempt to take a look at a few interesting exceptions whose remarkable contributions to the historical and cultural heritage of the subcontinent make for some compelling tales.

1

WILLIAM JONES

Rewriting Western Perceptions of India

> *'The Sanscrit language, whatever be its antiquity, is of a wonderful structure; more perfect than the Greek, more copious than the Latin, and more exquisitely refined than either, yet bearing to both of them a stronger affinity, both in the roots of verbs and the forms of grammar, than could possibly have been produced by accident; so strong indeed, that no philologer could examine them all three, without believing them to have sprung from some common source, which, perhaps, no longer exists; there is a similar reason, though not quite so forcible, for supposing that both the Gothic and the Celtic, though blended with a very different idiom, had the same origin with the Sanscrit; and the old Persian might be added to the same family.'*
>
> – William Jones[1]

August 1783

SIR WILLIAM JONES WAS IN THE PROCESS OF TAKING HIS EVENING walk aboard the quite fearsomely named ship – the *Crocodile.*

---

[1] From Jones's famous 'Third Anniversary Discourse' delivered to the Asiatic Society on 2 February 1786 (published in 1788 in Volume one of *Asiatic Researches*).

An hour's walk on the deck before dinner had been a part of his daily routine ever since the ship had left Portsmouth five months ago. A man of great energy and discipline, he had scrupulously organized his daily schedule in such a manner as to not waste a single waking hour on the long journey to India.

William and his new wife, Anna Maria Shipley, were on their maiden voyage to India. Anna Maria was sitting at the other end of the deck, reminiscing about the days, not long ago, when William was courting her. A highly accomplished woman, Anna was an artist and a poet who was proficient in both classical and modern languages. She was also interested in botany. What had initially attracted her to William was his refinement and scholarly bent of mind; his extraordinary philological skills had fascinated her. But she had come to value his kindness and humility even more.

Anna found her husband's obvious delight in her 'sweet society and conversation' endearing. Garland Cannon, in his *A Biography of Sir William Jones* published in 1960, mentioned that he had even admitted, in a letter to his friend Lord Althorp, that playing a game of chess with Anna Maria after dinner was his favourite recreation. Ever mindful of his new bride, William made sure he spent time with her every day, welcoming this pleasant addition to his routine.

Anna watched William fondly as he walked around on the deck. His face, framed by a shock of curly hair, made him look much younger than his 36 years. She could detect from his furrowed brow that his mind was ticking away, scheduling the subjects to be studied and researched to prepare himself for his trip to India. How very typical it was of William to be planning his future course of action and fretting about how much work lay ahead of him, while the other passengers were getting bored and grumbling about the long journey.

O.P. Kejariwal notes in his book, *The Asiatic Society of Bengal and the Discovery of India's Past, 1784-1838* published in 1988, that long before undertaking this journey, Jones had made a resolution to teach himself 'whatever relates to India', and had painstakingly created a memorandum titled, 'Objects of Enquiry during my residence in Asia' in preparation for the role he was to assume: a junior judge of the Supreme Court in Calcutta. In this note, he had listed those studies that would broaden the qualifications necessary for discharging the duties 'of his public station with satisfaction to himself and benefit to the community'. The list was hugely ambitious and included esoteric subjects such as:

- The Laws of the Hindus and Mohammedans
- The History of the *Ancient* World
- Proofs and Illustrations of Scripture
- Traditions concerning the Deluge
- Modern Politics and Geography of Hindustan
- Best mode of governing Bengal
- Arithmetic and Geometry, mixed Sciences of the Asiatics
- Medicines, Chemistry, Surgery and Anatomy of the Indians
- Natural Productions of India
- Poetry, Rhetoric and Morality of Asia
- Music of the Eastern Nations
- *The Shi King: The Old 'Poetry Classics' of the Chinese*

- Trade, Manufactures, Agriculture, and Commerce of India
- Moghul Constitution contained in the Desteri Alemghiri and *Ayein Acbari* (*Ain-i-Akbari* or the 'Constitution of Akbar')
- Mahratta Constitution
- The best accounts of Tibet and Cashmir (Kashmir)

As if there was not enough on his platter, Jones had kept aside a segment of his day to brush up his knowledge of Persian to prepare himself for his new role. Since Persian was the official language of the courts and proceedings in India, the knowledge of the language was crucial for a junior judge.

In August 1787, as recorded by A.J. Arberry his *Oriental Essays* published in 1960, Jones wrote a letter to Lord Althorp, his friend and pupil, stating that his single-point agenda was 'to know India better than any other European ever knew it'. And, incredible as it might seem, Jones far exceeded his objective. Not only would he succeed in that endeavour but he would one day be the leader of the band of Englishmen who 'discovered' India's past and initiated the resurgence of oriental studies in the West. The story of how he did it is a fascinating one.

William Jones was born in Westminster, London, on 20 September 1746 to Mary and William Nix Jones. His father, a well-known mathematician and a friend of Sir Isaac Newton, passed away when William was only three years old, leaving his family with moderate assets. Mary Jones was determined to give her son the best education in England and used up her limited assets to send him to Harrow School. He then studied at University College, Oxford. Jones proved to be a brilliant student and distinguished himself in classical scholarship and oriental languages, earning his Bachelor of Arts degree in 1768.

Jones displayed an extraordinary flair for languages from a very early age and was able to speak several languages. By the time he was 25, he had mastered Latin and Greek, and was composing verses in both. He was also fluent in French, German, Hebrew, Italian, Spanish, Portuguese and Chinese. While still at Oxford University, Jones also became proficient in Arabic and Persian, and wrote *A Grammar of the Persian Language*, before he arrived in India. Eventually, he would become proficient in 28 languages and be recognized as a super polyglot.

On 30 April 1772, in recognition of his accomplishment, Jones was elected as a Fellow of the Royal Society. However, Jones was practical enough to realize that oriental scholarship alone was not enough to make a living. Though it had brought him accolades, he also needed to enter a profession. Further, he could not propose marriage to his lady love without securing a job. Thus, he made up his mind to begin a legal career and joined the Middle Temple, a professional association for barristers in England and Wales, in 1770. Finally, in 1774, he was called to the Bar.

Even though law was not his chosen subject, Jones threw himself into the study of law with characteristic fervour and wrote a number of political papers, making a name for himself as a legal scholar. He even worked briefly with Benjamin Franklin, the legendary scientist and inventor who was also an author, political theorist, statesman, diplomat and one of the Founding Fathers of the United States.

Jones's passion for social justice, and his belief in righteousness and the fundamental rights of people is apparent from his wholehearted support of the American Revolution and his resistance to anti-people government regulations. So great was his conviction that he even wrote some political poems putting forth his views on government and morality, defending America and condemning Britain's war against America.

Unsurprisingly, by openly displaying his pro-American leaning and his Republican sympathies, Jones earned the disapproval of the British Tory Government. It might have been one of the reasons that he decided to go to India. And, because of his political clout, he had no difficulty in getting an appointment.

In March 1783, Jones attained the coveted appointment of junior judge of the Supreme Court in Calcutta and was consequently knighted soon after. For most Englishmen, relocation to India held a major attraction because it meant moving to a place where they could acquire great fortunes and return to England as 'nabobs'. In all fairness to Jones, though financial benefits might well have been an incentive, his interest in moving to India was the opportunity it allowed him to follow his first love: the study and research of the culture and languages of the people of the East.

Now, at last, he was in a position to propose to his beloved Anna Maria, which he did immediately. They were married in April 1783, and set sail for India that very month aboard the *Crocodile.*

William and Anna Jones had been on the ship for five months when one day they heard loud cheering from the passengers. The reason for the merriment was obvious – they had spotted the distant shores of India!

Franklin Edgerton, in his essay 'Sir William Jones', notes that Jones was filled with tremendous excitement – India, the country he had 'for so long and, so ardently, desired to visit', lay before him! It was in that moment when a happy thought struck him – he would now be experiencing, first-hand, all the 'eventful histories and agreeable fictions of this eastern world' he had so far only read in books.

The exhilaration and anticipation felt by Jones at that moment was expressed by him much later in the following words, documented by Arberry in his *Oriental Essays*:

> ...It gave me inexpressible pleasure to find myself in the midst of so noble an amphitheatre, almost encircled by the vast regions of Asia, which has ever been esteemed the nurse of sciences, the inventress of delightful and useful arts, the scene of glorious actions, fertile in the production of human genius, abounding in natural wonders...

Even more exciting for Jones was the thought that such an important and extensive field lay before him, 'yet unexplored'.

The first stop was Madras (now Chennai), where the passengers got their first taste of India. After a short break of a few days, they once more boarded the *Crocodile* and were on the way to their final destination.

They arrived in Calcutta (now Kolkata) by the end of September 1783. The Joneses took up residence in 8 Garden Reach, Calcutta, the place they would call home for the next 11 years. It was here that Jones's love for India, its people, culture and literature had a chance to flourish.

In December 1783, three months after reaching Calcutta, Jones began his legal career by addressing the grand jury. His oratorical powers were highly appreciated, and he impressed not just with his sincerity but also with his style of delivery, which was hailed as 'elegant, concise and appropriate', according to John Shore's *Memoirs of the Life, Writings and Correspondence, of Sir William Jones* published in 1806.

It needs to be mentioned here that Jones was not the first of the orientalists to arrive in India. By the time Jones arrived in Calcutta, some pioneering work had already begun in the field of oriental studies; the first ever translation (from Sanskrit into English) of the Bhagavad Gita and a section of the epic Mahabharata had already been done by Charles Wilkins, and the first Bengali grammar primer had been written and printed by his old friend from Oxford, Nathaniel Halhed. However, their work was not widely known since these early pioneers were working in isolation. From an early stage, Jones was convinced that the discovery of India's rich past and its culture could not be achieved by people working independently. The perusal of oriental studies needed to be a combined systematic effort. In his own words, 'Such inquiries and improvements could only be made through the united efforts of many, who are not easily brought, without some pressing inducement or strong impulse, to converge in a common point.'[2]

With this goal in mind, Jones began contacting friends and kindred souls soon after his arrival in Calcutta and sent

---

[2] From William Jones's 'A Discourse on the Institution of a Society for Inquiring into the History, Civil and Natural, the Antiquities, Arts, Sciences and Literature, of Asia' given on 15 January 1784.

out a formal letter putting forth his proposal for the creation of a society in India on the lines of the Royal Society of London.

There was an overwhelming response to Jones's epistle, and 30 European gentlemen belonging to the elite class got together on 15 January 1784 in the Grand Jury Room of the old Supreme Court of Calcutta. Thus, less than four months after his arrival in Calcutta, Jones succeeded in establishing the Asiatic Society of Bengal (initially named the Asiatick Society).

Sir William Jones's most important accomplishment in India was the establishment of this society, a unique institution that was to become the fountainhead for oriental studies and research. Indeed, it was a revolutionary event in the world of letters. The society was built on the belief that it was the East that held the secrets of early history and civilization of man, and that without the knowledge of the East, history of man could not be written. Ultimately, it was the society that brought to fruition Jones's aspiration to spread interest in oriental studies to the West.

The very first meeting of the society was presided over by Chief Justice Sir Robert Chambers. Governor-General Warren Hastings was elected its first president and Sir William Jones the vice-president. However, Hastings was in the midst of a court trial during that time following charges of misconduct and mismanagement. Since the case had stirred up a great deal of antagonism in England, Hastings felt that his alliance with the society would doom it to failure. Thus, he declined the appointment. Jones took over as president of the society on 5 February 1784 and held the post till his death in 1794.

In his inaugural address, Jones laid down the scope of inquiries proposed to be taken up by the society. He began by calling attention to the fact that it was a voluntary endeavour, not to be circumscribed by any rule – the only motivating factor being the 'love of knowledge'. The Memorandum of Articles of the society read as follows: 'The bounds of its investigations will be the geographical limits of Asia, and within these limits its enquiries will be extended to whatever is performed by MAN or produced by NATURE'. It was a memorable speech and brought out succinctly the ideals and vision that led Jones and inspired him in this extraordinary endeavour.

During his tenure as the president of the Asiatic Society, Jones delivered eleven anniversary discourses that highlight his contributions to the society's Asiatic research and mark a new era in the study of the Indian languages, literature and philosophy.

One of the things about Jones that mystifies scholars is that although he was a firm believer in the vital role of Sanskrit in the Aryan language family and its importance in learning about Hindu culture and literature, Jones himself did not show any urgency to learn Sanskrit in the initial stages. His own explanation for this was that his work load was too heavy for him to think of 'acquiring a new language'. But, more importantly, he felt he could depend on his close friend Charles Wilkins, who had already made quite a name for himself as a Sanskritist following his publication of the very first English translation of the Bhagavad Gita in 1785. Jones also felt secure in the knowledge that he could get Wilkins's help in any matter that might require the knowledge of Sanskrit. In fact, Edgerton notes, he had written to Wilkins saying, 'All my hopes therefore of being acquainted are grounded on the expectation of living to see the fruits of your learned labours'. But that was not to be. Wilkins fell sick, shortly after the publication of his translation the Bhagavad Gita, and was compelled to leave the country in 1785. Contrary to his fears, Wilkins's departure actually proved to be a turning point in Jones's career. Now that there was no one else he could turn to for guidance in problems requiring knowledge of Sanskrit, the need to learn the language became imperative. Especially since all the Hindu law books were written in Sanskrit. Besides, he realized that to do justice to his judicial work in India he had no choice but to learn the language.

Now began the search for someone who could teach him the language. But finding a teacher of Sanskrit was easier said than done. It turned out that the brahmin pandits – who were the sole repositories of the sacred language – were unwilling to impart their knowledge to a *mlechha* (from Vedic Sanskrit, *mlecchá*, meaning non-Vedic, foreign or barbarian) or non-believer.

Undeterred, Jones moved to Krishnagar, 60 miles from Calcutta. Krishnagar was considered to be the centre of Sanskrit learning in Bengal those days. But even there his efforts at finding a teacher were unsuccessful; it was festival season and, on his arrival, Jones found that the entire brahmin faculty had rushed home to celebrate Durga puja. Not to be put off, Jones persisted in his search. He succeeded in locating a teacher, at last, at the Nadia Hindu University by the name of Pandit Ramlochan.

Pandit Ramlochan Kavibhushana was a Vaidya, or physician, by caste. We understand through Cannon's *The Letters of Sir William Jones* published in 1970 that Jones was very happy with his teacher. He mentions in a letter that, though not a brahmin himself, Ramlochan had taught grammar and ethics to the learned brahmins.

Luckily, Sir William Jones was able to find a young Bengali assistant to help him communicate with his tutor in Sanskrit. Indeed, he writes in a letter to the second Earl of Spencer on 17 August 1787: 'I have employed a Brahman and a Bengal boy, who understands English, to translate the Sanscrit vocabulary; and they have already brought me ten thousand words; but things are my great object; since it is my ambition to know India better than any other European ever knew it.'

Jones describes Ramlochan as 'a pleasant old man of the medical caste who teaches me all he knows of the (Sanskrit) grammar'. Thus, with Ramlochan's assistance, he began the study of the Vedas and the classics. Soon, Jones became proficient in Sanskrit and began working on Kalidasa's *Shakuntala*, translating the Sanskrit classic to English in 1789, followed by his translation of Jaydeva's *Geet Govind* from Hindi to English in 1794. Jones translated *Manusmriti* from Sanskrit to English in 1794.

It was during the course of his studies that Jones made a startling discovery about Sanskrit. According to Edgerton's essay, he found that 'Sanskrit literature, like the language itself, was in every way the equal of Greek or Latin literature'. Even Shore, or hereafter Lord Teignmouth, in his previously mentioned biography of Jones, reveals that in a private letter to him Jones expressed his astonishment 'at the resemblance between that language [Sanskrit] and both Greek and Latin.' In 1786, Jones put forth his famous theory that, because Sanskrit had a strong resemblance to Greek and Latin, the three languages likely had a common parent language. He also suggested that they were related to the Gothic, Celtic and Persian languages.

On 2 February 1786, on the occasion of the third annual discourse of the Asiatic Society, Sir William Jones formally announced his remarkable conclusion to the European community, in the following speech:

> The Sanscrit language, whatever be its antiquity, is of a wonderful structure; more perfect than the Greek, more copious than the Latin, and more exquisitely refined than either, yet bearing to both of them a stronger affinity, both in the roots of verbs and the forms of grammar, than could possibly have been produced by accident; so strong indeed, that no philologer could examine them all three, without believing them to have sprung from some common source, which, perhaps, no longer exists; there is a similar reason, though not quite so forcible, for supposing that both the Gothic and the Celtic, though blended with a very different idiom, had the same origin with the Sanscrit; and the old Persian might be added to the same family.

This astounding finding created quite a stir in the Western world and was considered a significant discovery in the area of evolution of languages, as significant as the scientific discoveries of men like Galileo, Copernicus and Newton!

The great linguist Professor Suniti Kumar Chatterji, in her essay 'Sir William Jones', declared that, 'One may well say that the nature of linguistic development envisaged by the above sentences appeared in the mind of Sir William Jones with the flash of a prophetic inspiration.'

Soon after, Jones began investigating the dramatic literature of ancient India, of which next to nothing was known in Europe. He had heard about the Indian *natakas*, which were said to be a combination of history and fables. Further research revealed that *natakas* were actually popular works consisting of conversations in prose and verse to be performed before the king. It was Pandit Radhakant who explained to him that *natakas* were like the English plays performed in Calcutta during the cold season. Jones was thrilled when Radhakant introduced him to forgotten dramatic literature, particularly the fourth century *nataka* from the Gupta period called *Abhijnanasakuntalam*. Soon after, with the help of his teacher, Jones began reading this classic while simultaneously making a literal translation into Latin.

Jones was filled with incredulity at the treasure trove he had unearthed. With his background in classical studies, Jones knew at once that *Shakuntala* deserved to be recognized in world literature as a classic. To him Kalidasa was 'the Indian Shakespeare', according to Cannon's *Biography*. Jones now focused all his energy into translating his Latin version of *Shakuntala* into English. The English translation was published in Calcutta in 1789 as *Sacontalá or The Fatal Ring.* It was followed by publication in London in 1790 and in Edinburgh in 1796. The translated drama aroused unprecedented interest, taking the Western world by storm. The popularity of the book can be judged by the fact that it was reprinted thrice within seven years of its first publication in England.

Shakuntala was further translated into German, French and Italian. The German translation so impressed Goethe that he composed the following verse immortalizing *Shakuntala*:

Wouldst thou the young years blossom sand fruits of its decline
and all by which the soul is charmed,
enraptured, feasted, fed,

Would'st thou the earth and heaven
itself in one sole name combine?
I name thee, O Shakuntala! and all at once is said![3]

After Kalidasa's *Shakuntala*, Jones translated *Gita Govinda*, composed by the twelfth-century Indian poet Jayadeva. This was followed by *Hitopadesa*. These publications aroused tremendous interest in ancient Indian literature, particularly in the learned circles of Europe.

During the course of his translation work, realization dawned on Jones. While translating ancient Indian texts into English, European writers had been using the system known as transliteration, which is basically writing a letter or word by using the nearest letter from a different alphabet. Exploring these new languages, Jones was convinced that the 'Our English alphabet and orthography are disgracefully, and almost ridiculously, imperfect; and it would be impossible to express either *Indian*, *Persian* or *Arabic* words in *Roman* characters', as mentioned in the *Asiatic Researches* published in 1788. That is when he began to work on the standardization of transliteration.

---

[3] These lines are a translation from Johann Wolfgang von Goethe's German translation of *Shakuntala* by E.B. Eastwick.

Jones was amongst the earliest Englishmen to realize the importance of some sort of homogeneity in transliteration. Although some of the earlier Indologists had tried to develop some systems of orthography (the accepted way of spelling and writing words), Jones found several shortcomings in the system and set out to correct them. He did so by making *Devanagari* his standard language. This involved finding an equivalent Roman character for each letter of the *Devanagari* alphabet. His system remains valid even now. The outcome of his research was written in his paper titled 'A Dissertation on Orthography of Asiatic Words in Roman Letters'. This was his first contribution to the society's meeting.

Even before the printer's ink could dry, Jones had begun work in a very different area. He was now attempting to find a way of making Indian history more widely known. One needs to keep in mind that the major problem with Indian historiography had always been authentic historical writings – in the European sense of the term – which were non-existent before the advent of the Mughals.

Since there was no form of historical documentation to go by, Western historians had to often rely on the accounts of contemporary Greek and Roman writers to link the dates around which the history of India could be recreated. From J.S. Watson's translation of *Justin, Cornelius Nepos, and Eutropius* by Justin, the second century Latin historian, we learn that 'India...after the death of Alexander, had shaken, as it were, the yoke of servitude from its neck and put his governors to death. The author of this liberation was Sandrocottus'. The name of Sandrocottus is also mentioned by Megasthenes, the ambassador to Seleucus I, who was in India from 317 to 312 bce. He also refers to Palibothra as the capital of Sandrocottus's kingdom. The fact that Alexander had invaded India in the fourth century bce was well known, but the unanswered question was: who was Sandrocottus? And where exactly was Palibothra located?

These questions had remained unanswered for a long time. It was Jones who made the momentous breakthrough that Palibothra of the Greeks was actually Pataliputra, and Sandrocottus was none other than Chandragupta. Jones announced his discovery during a discourse on 'Asiatic History, Civil and Natural' in 1793. The story behind how he came to make these landmark discoveries is riveting.

It was while researching into contemporary Greek writings that Jones was struck by the fact that the Greeks had a penchant for changing the names of people and places according to their whims! According to Jones, as written in the *Asiatic Researches*, ancient Greeks were used to changing the actual words to what felt pleasant to their ears, and they appeared to have altered 'almost all the oriental names, which they introduced into their elegant, but romantic, histories'.

In 'A Dissertation on the Orthography of Asiatic words in Roman Letters', presented on 19 February 1784, Jones further elaborated that the ancient Greeks had '...strangely disguised the proper appellations of countries, cities, and rivers in Asia... They had a habit of moulding foreign names to a Grecian form and giving them a resemblance of some derivative word in their own tongue...'

This was a remarkable insight indeed and led to the identification of Chandragupta Maurya as Sandrocottus, the Indian king who had defeated Seleucus Nicator in a battle in 305 BCE, after Alexander's death in 323 BCE. According to Jones's 'Tenth Anniversary Discourse' given in 1793, 'the sovereign of upper Hindustan actually fixed the site of his empire at Pataliputra, where he received ambassadors from foreign princes, and was no other than that very Sandrocottus who concluded a treaty with Seleucus Nicator.'

The identification of Chandragupta had solved one riddle, but the question still remained: where was Pataliputra located? The confusion arose because Pataliputra was said to be located at the confluence of the rivers Ganges and Sone and extend up to Patna in some accounts, whereas in Megasthenes's account Pataliputra was located at the junction of the Ganges and a river named Errannoboas. Now, the main problem was the identification of Errannoboas. The confusion deepened when well-known scholar M. D'Anville and outstanding Scottish historian William Robertson claimed that Errannoboas was the Greek name for the river Yamuna. If they were to be believed, then the location of Palibothra would be present-day Allahabad!

The misunderstanding was ultimately cleared by Jones when he 'found in a classical Sanskrit book, nearly two thousand years old', the mention of Hiranyabahu (meaning 'golden-armed') as another name for the river Sone. Jones now had no doubt that Hiranyabahu was changed by the Greeks into Erannoboas, which meant 'the river with a lovely murmur'. Jones's conclusion was finally established when a brahmin scholar confirmed that, according to some ancient scriptures, the river Sone used to flow by Patna in ancient times, but had changed its course over the years and now flowed 25 miles west of Patna.

This discovery marked yet another milestone for Jones as it laid the foundation of ancient Indian chronology, as noted in the *Centenary Review of the Asiatic Society of Bengal* published in 1885:

> It renders it possible to synchronize the history of India with that of Greece at one point; and as the chronology of Greece is well known, we thus obtain a date in Indian chronology as a starting point, from which calculations may be made forwards and backwards with some degree of assurance.

***

It is said that law is a jealous mistress and bears no rival near her; but Jones proved this adage wrong by gaining tremendous success as not just a celebrated scholar but also a distinguished lawyer. It is difficult to comprehend how this multifaceted genius managed to pursue his numerous literary and academic interests with equal passion and still find the time and inclination to be an outstanding jurist.

There is no doubt that his democratic leanings and his belief in the fundamental rights of the people had impelled Jones to make law his lifelong career. He was convinced that in India good administration was not possible without a thorough mastery of the existing systems of law, and so he sought to have them codified and explained. 'My great object,' he wrote to Sir John Macpherson in 1786, the acting governor-general of Bengal, 'is to give our country a complete digest of Hindu and Musulman law', as recorded in Cannon's *Letters*. To achieve this, he embarked on a study and translation of the oldest Sanskrit law books. According to Lord Teignmouth, he aspired to be the Justinian of India, the great sixth-century Byzantine Emperor who created the Justinian Code that became the foundation of law in most western European countries.

Jones began preparing a complete digest of Hindu and Muhammadan laws as observed in India, gathering round him a team of learned native pandits and Muhammadan lawyers to assist him in this colossal labour. Around this time, Anna Maria's health, which had been delicate ever since their arrival in India, further deteriorated. Jones had to convince her to return to England. Anna Maria sailed for home that year. However, Jones felt duty-bound to stay back in India to complete his translation of the Hindu and Muslim laws. He hoped to return to England after the completion of his task and settle down in a pleasant country house.

As recorded by Arberry, Jones recalled with nostalgia in a letter to his friend that, 'This day ten years ago, we landed in Calcutta; and if it had not been for the incessant ill-health of my wife, they would have been the happiest years of a life always happy.' Whether he was in his Garden Reach bungalow in Calcutta or in a cottage in Nadia, Jones himself admitted that he had never been really happy till he settled in India. The only cloud that marred his contentment was his wife's ailment.

After Anna Maria's departure, Jones immersed himself in the study of the *Manusmriti*, or the 'Laws of Manu', one of the ancient legal texts of *Dharmaśāstra* (religious scriptures) of Hinduism. It is considered to be the most important and authoritative Hindu law books of ancient India. Jones's plan was to translate all 27 volumes of the original. Unfortunately, the climate of the country had started affecting his health too, and he was able to complete only seven volumes of the original text. These were put together and published in 1796 under the protracted title, *Institutes of Hindu Law: Or, the Ordinances of Menu, According to the Gloss of Culluca, Comprising the Indian System of Duties, Religious and Civil.*

Kejariwal in his 1988 book notes that Jones's efforts were recognized and lauded during the Asiatic Society centenary meeting in 1884, where it was stated, 'If Sir William Jones had done nothing else but translate the laws of Manu and invent a system of transliteration…he would have immortalized his name.' His other significant publications were the *Mahomedan Law of Succession to Property of Intestates*, and the *Al-Sirájiyyah: or Mohammedan Law of Inheritance.*

He decided to request the authorities for permission to return to England in 1795. But it was not to be. One evening in the month of April 1794, he complained of the onset of ague, an ailment with the same symptoms as malaria fever. Jones took it lightly, repeating an old proverb that 'an ague in the spring is medicine for a king'. However, it turned out to be an inflammation of the liver which had advanced too far by the time a physician was consulted. It proved fatal and Jones passed away on 27 April 1794, at the fairly young age of 47.

From his letter to a friend mentioned in Arberry's *Essays*, we are allowed a glimpse into what a day in Jones's life looked like: On a regular working day, Jones would rise an hour before the sun, walk three miles to the fort (Fort William); from there he would go in a palanquin to the courthouse where he would have a cold bath, dress up and have breakfast, and be ready by seven for his pandit, 'with whom I read Sanscrit. At eight come a Persian and Arab alternately with whom I read till nine; except on Saturday, when I give instructions to my Mughal secretary on my correspondence with my Musalman scholars. At nine come the attorneys with the affidavits: I am then robed and ready for the courts, where I sit on the bench, one day with another, five hours. At three I dress and dine; and till near sunset, I am at the service of my friends who choose to dine with me.' The hours after sunset were spent with Anna, reading together. They would go to bed by 10 p.m.

It was typical of the Joneses that despite such a packed schedule they managed to maintain an aura of serenity in their lives. Through John Keay's *India Discovered* published in 1981, we get an interesting glimpse of the near-pastoral life led by William and Anna Maria at home from a journal entry written by Thomas Twining, a 17-year-old employee of the East India Company who had been invited to dinner by Jones. Twining had heard so many stories about him that the young fellow had mentally prepared to expect the unexpected. His first surprise was probably the appearance of the host himself wearing a white Indian dress surmounted by a small black wig.

Twining writes in his journal that that Sir William 'was very cheerful and agreeable. He made some observations on certain mysterious words of Hindus and other subjects...' But the surprise of the evening came after dinner when his host 'suddenly called out in a loud voice "Othello, Othello!"' The young man was mystified as no one seemed to be attending his call, till at last he saw 'a black turtle of a very large size, crawling slowly towards us from an adjoining room. It made its way to the side of Sir William's chair...' The turtle was given some food that it seemed to like. Jones's love of nature and animals was further substantiated when, towards the end of the evening, 'this distinguished and able man' recited two lines of a Persian couplet that translated into English as: 'Kill not that ant, that steals a little grain: It lives with pleasure and it dies in pain.'

Shortly before his death, Jones had composed the following epitaph, evidently written for himself:

Here was deposited the mortal part of a man
who feared God but not death
and maintained independence
and sought not riches
who thought
none below him but the base and unjust
none above him but the wise and virtuous
who loved
his parents, kindred, friends, country
with an ardour
which was the chief source
of all his pleasures and his pains
and who having devoted his life to their service
and to
the improvement of his mind
resigned it calmly
giving glory to his creator
wishing peace on earth
and with
goodwill to all creatures

This epitaph reveals some striking features of Jones's personality and reflects Lord Teignmouth's assessment of Jones that he was 'totally free from pedantry, as well as from that arrogance and self-sufficiency that sometimes accompany and disgrace the greatest abilities; his presence was the delight of every society, which his conversation exhilarated and improved', as noted by Edgerton.

Ultimately, his greatest achievements were born out of a will to contribute to the world around him. Henry Roscoe in his 1841 book *Lives of Eminent British Lawyers* said that, 'The crowning virtue of Sir William Jones's character was his pure and ardent desire to benefit mankind. In this great ambition, every meaner passion was forgotten. To this shrine he carried all the rich offerings of his taste, his learning, and his genius.'

Jones was loved and respected by all classes of people, both amongst his compatriots and Indians. Lord Teignmouth speaks rapturously about the cordiality of his conversation, behaviour and his modest, unassuming manners. He asserts that Jones's interaction 'with the Indian natives of character and abilities was extensive: he liberally rewarded those by whom he was served and assisted, and his dependents were treated by him as friends'.

The love and reverence Jones evoked amongst the people who worked with him is evident from the reaction of the pandits on learning of his demise. Jones's biographer further writes that when he saw the pandits at a public durbar 'a few days after that melancholy event, [they] could neither restrain their tears for his loss, nor find terms to express their admiration at the wonderful progress which he had made in the sciences which they professed'.

Jones's greatest contribution was in making the world aware of the existence of ancient languages and cultures in India dating back to centuries ago; far older and richer than Western culture. He not only introduced the Western world to the rich heritage of India but also precipitated the Romantic movement in the West through his writings. His unique style of writing, which combined Western and Eastern elements, deeply influenced poets like Samuel Taylor Coleridge and Lord Byron. His literary works also impacted several poets, writers and thinkers, including Johann Wolfgang von Goethe, Ralph Waldo Emerson, T.S. Eliot, Matthew Arnold, Walt Whitman and Rudyard Kipling.

Jones's writings, unlike many of his contemporaries, do not display the Eurocentric prejudices prevalent during his time; nor did he subscribe to the contemporary trend of interpreting the histories and cultures of oriental societies from a Western perspective. He rejected the view of the German scholars who subscribed to the theory of the Vedanta to be the unique manifestation of 'Aryan genius', instead he stressed its similarity with other works of philosophy. In his view, as noted in Jones's *Memoir* by Lord Teignmouth, one could not 'read the Vedanta...without believing Pythagoras and Plato derived their sublime theories from the same fountain with the sages of India.'

Jones achieved the seemingly impossible task of making oriental studies attractive to Western scholars by reshaping their perception of India. But perhaps even more significant was the fact that his contributions helped Indians to rediscover their own heritage and understand the lost glory of their past.

David Kopf, a research scholar on South Asian history, mentions in his book *British Orientalism* and the *Bengal Renaissance* published in 1969 that Jones's most important accomplishment was that he 'reanimated the resplendent Hindu past'. Kopf accorded him the greatest honour of all when he credited Jones with restoring India to her rightful place among the civilizations of the world by rediscovering her golden age of arts and letters.

2

SIR CHARLES WILKINS

A Mechanics and Literary Genius

'See patient Wilkins to the world unfold.
Whate'er discovered the Sanskrit relics hold,
But he performed a yet more noble part
He gave to Asia typographic art.'
– *The Asiatic Annual Register*, 1801

1788

CHARLES WILKINS LOOKED OVERWHELMED AS HE HELD THE BOOK delivered to him from the printer. Its title read *A Grammar of the Bengal Language* by Nathaniel Brassey Halhed. Above and below the English title was a description in Bengali font. Wilkins's eyes scanned the title of the book, not for the English text, but the Bengali translation that accompanied it.

His face brightened. Yes, the font was just right! He then quickly flipped through the pages, glancing at the design, the types and the font. A long sigh of relief escaped him.

He had done it!

A dramatic moment indeed. It was the very first book to be printed in the Bengali language. The book, which has a large section written in the Bengali script, had been authored by his friend Halhed. But it was Wilkins who had designed the Bengali type and font, without which the book would never have been printed.

It was a defining moment, not just in the life of Wilkins but also in the history of printing in India. By preparing the earliest known set of Bengali type font, this young employee of the East India Company had, at the age of 28, become the first man to print in a vernacular language in India. And, thanks to Wilkins, Bengali became the first Indian language to appear in print.

This achievement alone would have secured Wilkins a place in history, but it was just the beginning of a long list of astounding achievements that would establish him as a part of the British triumvirate of oriental scholars, along with William Jones and James Prinsep.

Unlike Jones and other contemporary orientalists, Wilkins came from an impoverished family of clothiers. If he had any education at all, it was erratic. Yet, despite lacking a formal college education, Wilkins became renowned as the first Sanskrit scholar from England and revealed to the world the hidden treasures of India.

Charles Wilkins was born in 1749 to Walter Wilkins and Martha Wray at Frome in Somerset, a rural county in England. Not much is known of his early life apart from the miserable conditions of his childhood and his dream of getting away. However, it has been established that Robert Bateman Wray, a noted engraver and printer of England, was his mother's uncle and that young Charles trained with him. In all probability, this same granduncle also helped him get his first appointment in India.

Charles arrived in Calcutta in July 1770 at the age of 21. After his arrival, he was appointed to the position of a writer in the junior civil service of the East India Company and worked in this position for two years. Even as a junior employee at the time, Charles was smart enough to realize that to be an effective administrator it was crucial for government servants to acquire a knowledge of the local languages.

The East India Company College (later renamed Haileybury College) prepared young men to become clerks for the East India Company. Besides the wide curriculum of subjects, it was compulsory to learn Sanskrit, Persian and Hindustani, while other languages including Arabic, Bengali, Telugu, Hindi and Marathi were optional. When Wilkins was enrolled in the college, merely picking up the basics of the languages was not enough for him. And so he began spending his leisure time trying to master Bengali, Hindi and Persian. Having a great aptitude for languages he soon mastered all three. This turned out to be providential, as it helped him get his next job.

In 1781, he was appointed as the translator for Bengali and Persian in the revenue department of the East India Company, and also as superintendent of the Company's press. During this time, with the assistance of a pandit and munshi, he was successful in translating a royal inscription in Kutila characters, a script that dates back to 992 CE and had remained indecipherable till then.

Wilkins was next transferred to Malda, another district within Bengal. At that time, Malda was a flourishing township and a business hub of Bengal, and the Company had established many factories there. Wilkins was employed as assistant of the superintendent of one of the Company's factories. The job gave him a lot of free time, which he utilized to brush up on his Persian and Bengali, the two most common languages in use. During this time, Charles became good friends with Nathaniel Halhed, a compatriot and fellow employee of the East India Company. This friendship turned out to be extraordinarily beneficial for both of them.

Halhed was a philologist with a good knowledge of the Bengali and Persian languages. He had distinguished himself in 1776 for his translation of an ancient text on Hindu law, *Code of Gentoo Laws*. This set of legal code was first translated from Sanskrit into Persian by brahmin scholars and from Persian to English by Halhed. He had also compiled a Bengali grammar primer and sought Wilkins's help to have it published.

It seemed an impossible task at that time, as vernacular printing was non-existent and Bengali typefaces had not even been developed. Although a few Bengali books had been printed before 1778, those were in Roman font. In the 1770s, a judge in Calcutta by the name of William Bolts had provided a London printer with designs for a Bengali font of type to facilitate East India Company publications. However, the result was most unsatisfactory, and the project had to be dropped.

A serendipitous occurrence at this time set the ball rolling once more. Warren Hastings, the first governor-general of India, was keenly interested in the project. In 1778, he asked Wilkins to prepare a set of Bengali types for Halhed's *A Grammar of the Bengal Language*. Wilkins took up the job of printing Halhed's book with great alacrity. Assisted by Joseph Shepherd, a well-known engraver, and Panchanan Karmakar, a Bengali blacksmith and typesetter, he set up as an amateur printer. Wilkins's early experience in typecasting in England came in handy and he was able to use his skill in engraving, designing, casting and setting the first Bengali types. In the words of Halhed in the preface of the *Grammar*, 'with a rapidity unknown in Europe, he [Wilkins] surmounted all the obstacles which necessarily clog the first rudiments of a difficult art as well as disadvantages of solitary experiment.'

Wilkins successfully published Halhed's *A Grammar of the Bengal Language* in 1778, probably from Endorse Press in Hoogly. He thus became the first man to print in a vernacular language, thereby representing the first successful reproduction of the Bengali language in metal type. Though Halhed's *Grammar* is widely recognized as the first grammar book of the Bengali language, there are those who claim that the first was written by a Portuguese monk and published three decades earlier. Nevertheless, Halhed's *Grammar* was widely appreciated and hailed as a typographical masterpiece.

Wilkins proved to be an enthusiastic and dedicated partner throughout the project. He voluntarily took upon himself all the different jobs required for this complex task. Halhed alludes to this in his preface: 'he has been obliged to charge himself with all the various occupations of the metallurgist, the engraver, the foundry man and the printer. ...he surmounted all the obstacles which necessarily clog the first rudiments of a difficult art as well as disadvantages of solitary experiment.'

Spurred by the success of this project, Wilkins followed up by casting a font of Persian types, which was used for many years to print a handbook of regulations for the employees of the East India Company. This development had a tremendous impact in Asia, and Wilkins was hailed as the Caxton of India, after William Caxton, the first Englishman to introduce the printing press to England. The East India Company placed Wilkins in charge of their press, where government documents in Persian and Bengali were also printed. The colonial government, which until then had no press for Indian languages, now began to publish its Bangla publications from his printing press. A direct outcome of Wilkins's success was the publication of the very first newspaper in India, *Hicky's Bengal Gazette or the Original Calcutta General Advertiser*, published by James Augustus Hicky. The inaugural issue of the paper popularly referred to as *Hicky's Gazette* appeared on 29 January 1780.

Wilkins had no plans to rest on his laurels. He had set a much higher objective for himself. His next goal was to learn Sanskrit, the sacred language of the Hindus. In fact, his association with Halhed had a profound effect on him and inspired him to take his studies to another level. Wilkins noted, in his book *A Grammar of the Sanskrĭta Language* published in 1808, that in 1778 'my curiosity was excited by the example of my friend, Mr Halhed, to commence the study of the Sanskrit.' Wilkins was fully aware that Sanskrit, 'though no longer a spoken tongue', was of importance because it contained 'the books of their [the ancient Indians] religion and law and forming the source of most of the modern dialects of the sub-continent'.

However, it proved to be difficult. One of the major difficulties in learning the language at that time was that the grammatical treatises were themselves composed in Sanskrit. So, unless a person was already well-versed in Sanskrit, he could not study Sanskrit grammar! Finding a teacher to instruct him in Sanskrit turned out to be an even more difficult task. Being the only persons acquainted with the textual traditions of India, the brahmins guarded this privilege zealously and were loath to teach the language to any non-brahmin. The reason given was that by providing instructions to a *mlechha*, they would run the risk of facing expulsion from their caste.

It is doubtful if Wilkins would have succeeded without the help of the governor-general of India himself. Luckily for him, Warren Hastings had been suitably impressed by Wilkins's adeptness at Indian languages. Hastings was instrumental in arranging for him to go to Benares (now Varanasi) and learn Sanskrit under the tutorship of a reputed Sanskrit scholar by the name of Kashinath Bhattacharya. In fact, the governor-general had even arranged for Wilkins to be given a leave of absence from his duties at the Company to continue his studies at Benares Kashi.

According to his contemporaries, Wilkins's house in Benares soon became 'the resort of the learned men of Kashi', as noted by Rajesh Kochhar in his 2021 book *Sanskrit and the British Empire.* Wilkins was deeply influenced by his associations with the pandits in Benares and began to prepare for his mammoth project of translating the Mahabharata, the great Hindu epic, into English. It was a voluminous undertaking and, despite giving all his time to it, he was not able to complete the entire translation. However, with the encouragement of Warren Hastings, he was able to complete translating the most important section of the epic – the Bhagavad Gita, the dialogue between the incarnate Lord Krishna and his pupil Arjun. Wilkins completed the translation of the Bhagavad Gita in November 1784.

Later that year, Hastings visited Benares. He was so pleased with Wilkins's work that he sent it to the Court of Directors, the executive branch of the East India Company, requesting them to publish and advertise it – which they did. The Court of Directors went on to print it at their own expense under the title *The Bhagvat-Geeta, Or Dialogues of Kreeshna and Arjoon in Eighteen Lectures*. The book was published by Nourse, the famous printing press in Central London, in 1785.

The publication was a landmark event as *Bhagvat-Geeta* was the first translation of a Sanskrit work into a European language based directly on a Sanskrit text. Numerous copies of the book were distributed to libraries and educational institutions across Europe. The translation of the Bhagavad Gita, described as the 'quintessence of Hindu philosophy and religion' by K.S.S. Seshan in an article in *The Hindu*, proved to have a major influence on Romantic literature. More importantly, it had a far-reaching influence on the European understanding of Hinduism.

So impressed was Warren Hastings by this work that he presented a copy of the *Bhagvat-Geeta* to the chairman of the East India Company and, as noted in his preface to the book, introduced it as 'a performance of great originality, of a sublimity of conception, reasoning and diction; almost unequalled, and single exception among all the known religions of mankind of a theology accurately corresponding with that of the Christian dispensation and most powerfully illustrating its fundamental doctrines'. Hastings concluded with a prophetic statement in his preface: 'The writers of the Indian philosophies will survive when the British Dominion in India shall long have ceased to exist, and when the sources which it yielded of wealth and power are lost to remembrance.' Thus, 'this jewel of Hindu literature and learning, became known and appreciated, all over the far West'.

William Blake, the English poet, painter and printmaker who was a pioneer of Romanticism, celebrated the publication in a drawing titled *The Bramins.* The now lost drawing, which was exhibited in 1809, depicts Charles Wilkins working on his translation of the Gita along with a group of brahmins.

The publication of Wilkins's Gita made a huge impact in Europe as well as America, and it inspired translations of the Gita into other European languages. In 1787, there appeared a French version. This was followed by a Russian and a German translation over the next few years. Wilkins's translation also inspired quite a few scholars to study Sanskrit themselves. The German philosopher and the first German Sanskritist, Friedrich von Schlegel (1772–1829), translated extracts from the Gita directly from Sanskrit into German in 1808, while another Schlegel from Germany – Wilhelm von Schlegel – translated it to Latin in 1823, printing the original in Devanagari script alongside the Latin translation.

Wilkins's other great passion was epigraphy, the science of decoding ancient inscriptions and analysing their contents. Studies in Indian epigraphy had already begun in the eighteenth century and was seriously taken up by many orientalists.

Along with his translation work, Wilkins had also been occupied with interpreting the ancient inscriptions carved on rocks and temple walls. It was only in 1781 that Wilkins succeeded in deciphering and translating an inscription engraved on a copper plate found in Munger in present-day Bihar. Further research revealed that the origin of this inscription could be traced to Vigrahapala, the fifth king of the Pala dynasty in Bengal. This was followed by the discovery of another monument of the Pala period – the Budal pillar belonging to Narayanapala in Dinajpur district.

Later, Wilkins tackled the Gopika Cave inscription, also called the Nagarjuni Hill Cave inscription. These were dedications inscribed by King Anantavarman of the Maukhari dynasty, a post-Gupta dynasty that held sway over a major part of northern India for over six generations. The inscriptions were in Sanskrit and Kutila, both early version of Devanagari characters. These epigraphic assessments led to discoveries of the Pala and Maukhari dynasties.

These discoveries were published by the Asiatic Society as *Asiatic Researches* in 1788 and 1790 respectively. The pioneering work done by Wilkins in this area aided historians in their reconstruction of ancient history.

As with many of his compatriots, Wilkins found that India's extreme climate as well as his unremitting hard work had begun to affect his health. He was compelled to go back to England in 1786. Soon after returning home, he married Elizabeth Keeble. A year later, Wilkins produced a translation of *Hitopadesha*, a collection of Sanskrit fables in prose and verse, under the title *The Heettopades of Veeshnoo-Sarma*.

He was elected a fellow of the Royal Society in 1786. Sadly, Wilkins's wife died after the birth of their second daughter in 1788. He married Lucky Shingler the following year, and a third daughter was born in 1790. During his return to England, Wilkins had taken back with him rare Sanskrit texts that he had collected in India. Unfortunately, along with his home in Kent, all these precious manuscripts were destroyed in a huge fire in 1796. However, Wilkins was not a man to easily accept defeat. He started afresh from where he had left off, and continued to pursue both his literary and mechanical interests.

Soon he resumed working on his pet project and devoted himself to the creation of a font for Devanagari script used in Sanskrit. The script is also used in more than a 100 other languages, like Hindi, Bhojpuri, Bihari, Marathi, Kashmiri, Sindhi, Bhili and Konkani, making it one of the most used writing systems in the world. The creation of this typeface gave a big boost to the Indian publishing industry.

In 1800, the East India Company decided to place Wilkins in charge of the large collection of manuscripts that had been found after capturing Seringapatam and other places, which were housed in the India House Library (now British Library – Oriental Collections). During this period he wrote many erudite papers on Indian subjects. He was also appointed visitor of Haileybury, the East India Company College, and Addiscombe, the East India Company Military Seminary or the British military academy at Surrey, in the Oriental Department.

Wilkins never forgot the initial hardship he faced in 1776 because of the absence of any grammatical treatises for

Sanskrit (besides those written in Sanskrit). Thus, he fulfilled a long-cherished wish by publishing his book *A Grammar of the Sanskrita Language* in 1808 for the benefit of the East India Company College. The grammar attempts to explain the language, logically and coherently. For a long time, it was considered an essential resource in bringing Indian languages within the reach of the English-speaking public. Wilkins followed this up by editing the first volume of a new edition of John Richardson's Persian and Arabic dictionary, the second volume of which appeared in 1810.

In 1825, Oxford University awarded Wilkins with an honorary doctorate in Civil Law. In the same year, the Royal Society of Literature presented him with their medal inscribed with the words 'Princeps Literature Sanskrita', a Latin phrase meaning the distinguished or most eminent person of Sanskrit Literature. He was knighted in 1833, in recognition of his services to oriental scholarship.

Sir Charles Wilkins passed away in London on 13 May 1836 at the age of 86. He will always be remembered for his outstanding contribution in lifting the veil on India's past, and for giving the world its first glimpse of India's ancient culture and history.

3

NATHANIEL BRASSEY HALHED

The Pioneer of Modern Philology

'When we read in the valuable production of those great Oriental scholars...those of a Jones, a Wilkings, a Colebrooke, or a Halhed, – we uniformly discover in the Hindus a nation, whose polished manners are the result of a mild disposition and an extensive benevolence.'

– Francis Buchanan in 'Buchanan's Travel's in the Mysore', 1809

22 August 1819, London

NATHANIEL BRASSEY HALHED WAS SITTING IN HIS STUDY IN isolation, overcome by taedium vitae. This feeling of worldly weariness had begun soon after his departure from India and had engulfed him completely following the death of his mentor and inspiration, Warren Hastings. Halhed had not indulged in any intellectual or literary activity since his return to London.

It seemed only yesterday that the world was waxing eloquent about his *Bengali Grammar*, the first-ever book to be written on the Bengali language, and his translation of the Hindu Law books into English had been extolled by critics. The 1777 issue of the *Critical Review* issue in London had described *A Code of Gentoo Laws* as 'a most sublime performance'. Yes, he had reached the pinnacle of success. And yet, there he was, at the age of 68, all but forgotten by the world; the very world that had applauded him and eulogized his literary work.

Fate had bestowed on him affluence, social success and friends in high places, besides outstanding scholarship and undisputed talent. Success and recognition had come to him early in life. Even before he had turned 30, he had won kudos all over Europe as an orientalist and philologist. Yet, perhaps because of his philandering way of life or maybe the wrong choices he had made, he was now left without a job and in abject poverty. While his peers in the East India Company continued their intellectual activities right till the ends of their lives, Halhed, after a display of amazing brilliance and promise in his twenties, had dissipated his energies in romantic indulgences, involvement in political issues and neo-religious movements.

Nathaniel Brassey Halhed was born in Westminster on 25 May 1751. He was the eldest son of William Halhed, a long-time director of the Bank of England, and Frances Caswall, the daughter of the late John Caswall, an MP for Leominster.

Born into a well-to-do family, Halhed studied at Harrow School from the age of seven. In 1768, at the age of seventeen, he was admitted to Christ Church, one of the largest colleges in Oxford University. While in college, Halhed met some eminent people who would profoundly influence his life, including William Jones who inspired him to learn Persian and Arabic.

Halhed's remarkable poetic talent also brought him in contact with Richard Brinsley Sheridan, the eminent writer and dramatist. A close friendship developed between the two, and they collaborated on a number of literary projects. Initially they worked on *Crazy Tales,* probably a clever imitation of a licentious production popular at the time, and another farce called *Ixion* (the name was later changed to *Jupiter*). However, their most well-known and most controversial work was *The Love Epistles of Aristaenetus,* translated from Greek into English metre by Halhed and revised by Sheridan.

The book, which was published anonymously, soon became the talk of the town. Initially it received good reviews, but after some time, the book was severely criticized following a controversy over its authorship. It was being said that the idea for the book might have been Halhed's but was actually written by Sheridan. Though the rumours were proved to be false, it was the beginning of a crack in their friendship. Soon it turned into a full-blown rivalry when both Halhed and Sheridan fell in love with the same woman: the beautiful concert artist Elizabeth Linley, the daughter of Thomas Linley, a well-known composer of the time.

Elizabeth initially raised Halhed's hopes by bestowing her favours on him. He was deeply infatuated by her after hearing her sing for the very first time at Oxford. Soon after, Linda Kelly notes in her book *Richard Brinsley Sheridan: A*

Life published in 2012, he wrote to Sheridan, 'I am petrified, my faculties are annihilated with wonder. My conception could not form such a power of voice – such melody – such a soft yet audible a tone.' Halhed wrote a number of letters to Sheridan detailing his obsession for Elizabeth. However, it seems that Sheridan at that time did not reveal to his friend that she had already committed herself to him. One can imagine what a shock it was for Halhed when Elizabeth ditched him and married Sheridan.

Deeply dejected following this turn of events, Nathaniel decided to leave the country and applied for a job in India. His father, who was disappointed for his son, was also keen to get him out of the country and used his influence with Harry Verelst, the former governor of Bengal, to get Nathaniel a writership in the service of the East India Company. Halhed arrived in Calcutta in 1772 and began working as a writer in the accountant general's office under one Mr Darrel.

After some time, he was transferred to the office of the Persian translator in Kasimbazar, where he got the opportunity to strengthen his knowledge of Persian. While in Kasimbazar, he also got the opportunity to pick up Bengali, which, as we shall see later, proved to be a boon for him.

It is interesting to note that unlike Jones and Wilkins, Halhed's initial reaction on coming to India was that of total disenchantment. Back home in London, he had heard stories of how Englishmen could make easy money in India and amass immense wealth within a short time without any effort. Money thus earned was euphemistically referred to as shaking the pagoda tree. Pagoda refers to the gold coin being minted by many Indian dynasties during eighteenth and nineteenth century, and alludes to the image of a *gopuram* carried by the South India gold coins of the time.

To Brassey's chagrin, the pagoda tree had dried up. Within two years of his arrival, Halhed was ready to throw in the towel and return to England. The extent of his disappointment can be gauged from a letter he wrote on 5 November 1773 to a former classmate at Harrow by the name of Samuel Parron:

> India (the wealthy, the luxurious, and the lucrative) is so exceedingly ruined and exhausted, that I am not able by any means, not with the assistance of my education in England, and the exertion of all my abilities here, to produce even a decent subsistence. I have studied the Persian language with the utmost application in vain; I have courted employment without effect; and after having suffered much, from the heat of the climate, spent whatever money I had brought into the country, and seen the impossibility of providing for myself for some years to come...

He ended the letter by saying that he had taken the resolution of '*quitting so disagreeable a spot*, before the necessity of running deeply into debt confines me here for years (perhaps for life).'

However, better sense seems to have prevailed. Halhed, known to be an extremely sensitive person, tried to shake off his despondence by reviving his penchant for poetry. He now began amusing himself by composing humorous verses that painted vivid pictures of the lives of British expatriates in Bengal during his time. One of the poems that became very popular was *A Lady's Farewell to Calcutta*, a lament for those who were unhappy about staying in the *mofussil* (districts outside an urban centre).

Interestingly, despite his miserable plight, he did not give up on his dalliances and continued his romantic affairs in Bengal. As noted by Rosane Rocher in her 1983 book *Orientalism, Poetry, and the Millenium*, he used his poetic talent to write odes in the form of amorous lyrics and supplication to, and had liaisons with, several European women of Calcutta, including Elizabeth Pleydell, a certain Nancy, Diana Rochfort and Henrietta Yorker, among others.

After indulging in a number of amorous peccadilloes, Halhed eventually met and proposed to Helena Louisa Ribaut. She was the stepdaughter of Johannes Matthias Ross, who was the head of the Dutch factory at Kasimbazar during his tenure there. There are no records of the nuptials. It is most likely that they took place in 1775. Though it is believed that the marriage was a little rocky in the beginning, later their bond became very strong. Helena remained a pillar of support during the last and most difficult phase of Halhed's life. They never had any children.

To get a better perspective of Halhed's career in India, we need to go back to the time when he first came to this country. It was a period when the political situation was undergoing a major overhaul. The Court of Directors had informed the president and council at Fort William College about the assumption of the Diwani by the East India Company. This meant that the Company gained the right to collect revenues and decide civil cases. Thus, around the time when Halhed was appointed as writer, the administration of civil justice was handed over to Warren Hastings, the newly appointed governor-general, who took charge in April 1772.

Halhed's obvious literary talent and his academic background in Harrow and Christ College attracted the attention of the new governor-general. Soon Halhed became one of Hastings's favourites, and in turn was one of his most loyal supporters. This relationship was, as we shall see, also the cause of Halhed's ultimate downfall...but that comes later.

Hastings firmly believed that it was imperative for the British rulers to apply the native laws on their subjects rather than impose British laws that were totally alien to them. Following his conviction, he submitted the Judicial Plan of 1772 within a few months of taking charge. The plan stated: 'all suits regarding the inheritance, marriage, caste and other religious usages, or institutions, the laws of the Koran with respect to Mohametans (Muslims) and those of the Shaster (shastra) with respect to Gentoos shall be invariably adhered to.'[1]

Hastings's plan to produce an English version of the native laws was no doubt inspired by his wish to reconcile British rule with Indian institutions but at the same time, he also wished to show his compatriots that India was not the savage state that many in the West believed it to be. Also, Hastings understood very well that to accomplish his aim of establishing the authority of the British government in Bengal on its ancient laws, it was essential for European judges to familiarize themselves with the ancient laws of the country. Hastings put Halhed in charge of this project.

---

[1] As stated by Warren Hastings on 15 August 1772. Recorded in the *Selections from the State Papers of the Governors-general of India* edited by G.W. Forrest, published in 1910.

This proved to be the defining moment in Halhed's career. In choosing Halhed to direct this project, Hastings 'cured (Halhed) of his aimless dissipation', according to M.J. Franklin in his essay 'Cultural Possession, Imperial Control, and Comparative Religion'. We see the first signs of change in his life during this period. Halhed was now putting all his energy into fulfilling this undertaking.

Soon, under the supervision of the governor-general, the mammoth project got underway. It was a long and complex process, as the ancient Indian legal code *Vivādārṇavasetu* had to be first translated from Sanskrit to Bengali, which in turn would be translated to Persian (a language both Halhed and Hastings knew well), and then finally into English.

It began with the appointment of 11 brahmin pandits to work daily on compiling a Bengali oral version of a digest of Hindu law books in Sanskrit. The oral version was then put down in Bengali text by a Bengali clerk and translated into Persian by Zaid ud-Din 'Ali Rasa'. The work began sometime after Warren Hastings became the first Governor General of India in 1773 and the text was completed in 1775. When the Persian text was ready, it was translated into English by Halhed. The English version was titled *Vivadarnavasetu, or the Sea of Litigations*, and had a preface by Halhed.

The translation was handed over to Hastings on 27 March 1775 and was printed in London in 1776 under the title *A Code of Gentoo Laws, or, Ordinations of the Pundits*. The publication got enthusiastic support from the governor-general. Hastings was so enthusiastic about the book that he sent sections of the translation to the Company of Directors even while the book was in the process of being written. According to Rocher, he gave a glowing review of the book, ending with the statement, '… I have been earnest in transmitting these sheets for your information, as they will afford at least a proof that the people of this country do not require our aid to furnish them with a rule for their conduct, or a standard for their propriety.'

Initially, the digest was not in the market for sale and copies of the book were distributed by the East India Company. *A Code of Gentoo Laws, or, Ordinations of the Pundits* gained instant recognition, and according to a contemporary review in the London-based *Critical Review* in September 1771:

> Mr Halhed has rendered more real service to this country, to the world in general, by this performance, than ever flowed from all the wealth of all the nabobs by whom the country of these poor people has been plundered... Wealth is not the only, nor the most valuable commodity, which Britain might import from India.

Its popularity can be judged from the fact that within a year, a pirated edition of the book was in circulation; followed by a second edition in 1781. And, by 1778 the book had been translated into French and German, and was selling successfully all over Europe. As a result, Halhed became a celebrity while still in his twenties. The publication was highly acclaimed and praise poured in. William Robertson, the well-known Scottish historian and minister in the Church of Scotland as well as the principal of the University of Edinburgh, hailed Halhed's work and praised it as the 'most valuable and authentic elucidation of Indian policy and manners that has been hitherto communicated to Europe' in his 1835 book *An Historical Disquisition Concerning the Knowledge which the*

Ancients Had of India. Fortunately for Halhed, Robertson was known for his conscious effort to move away from a Eurocentric approach and write with empathy of the civilization of the Indian sub-continent.

However, it was probably inevitable that along with bouquets came brickbats. Some scholars doubted the reliability of a book that was translated twice. William Jones was the first one to question the credibility and authenticity of the text, remarking that third-degree translation was likely to be erroneous, highly flawed and not conforming to the original. 'Indeed, we cannot call it a translation,' he wrote, as recorded in *The Asiatic Journal and Monthly Register* in 1828, 'for though Mr Halhed performed his part with fidelity, yet the Persian interpreter had supplied him only with a loose injudicious epitome of original Sanscrit, in which abstract many essential passages are omitted, though several notes of little consequence are interpolated...' It must be mentioned here that Jones himself (while working on his own translations) used to translate the Sanskrit text into Latin first and then from Latin into English.

Another scholar by the name of John Dawson Mayne was rather harsh in his criticism of the 'translation of a translation' in his publication *Treatise on Hindu Law and Usage* from 1878, calling it a work of poor quality. Though the book never made it as the authoritative text of the Anglo-Indian judicial system, it cannot be denied that Halhed's *Code of Gentoo Laws* earned its place in Indian history as the very first attempt to codify Hindu law in English.

The book also made the British judges aware of the need to consider existing Hindu laws while pronouncing a judgment. More importantly, Halhed's erudite preface of the book lifted the veil on Hindu customs, traditions, history and law, and paved the way for a number of illustrious scholars and orientalists who came after him.

We must keep in mind that Halhed, who had arrived in India more than a decade before Jones, was the first European to detail in English the structure of Sanskrit as a language that, stated in *Gentoo Laws*, 'far exceeds the Greek and Arabic in the regularity of its etymology, and like them has a prodigious number of derivatives from each primary root.' Halhed took this theory further when he began working on *A Grammar of the Bengal Language* that would be published after about two years. He writes in the preface about 'the similitude of Shanscrit words with those of Persian and Arabic and even of Latin and Greek'. In his theory about the relationship of Sanskrit with other classical languages of the world, Halhed anticipates Jones's 'Third Anniversary Discourse' of 1786.

At the time Halhed arrived in Bengal, British officials had no knowledge of the Bengali language. This was proving to be an obstacle for the East India Company officials in their dealings with the weavers of Bengal. For a long time, the language barrier had been the biggest hurdle for the British administration in their trade with the *aurangs* (the local centres of manufacturing production). Although the government realized the importance of employing good translators for any meaningful communication with the peasants, they could find no suitable person to take on the task.

Halhed, who by now had become quite well versed in the Bengali language, volunteered to take on the responsibility for bringing out the first Bengali grammar book. In this effort he received complete support from the governor-general, who paid the salaries of the pandits and the scribe who assisted Halhed in the project.

The text was soon ready; but the big question was, how was the book to be printed? The manuscript could not be sent to England for printing because the book, though written in English, had used extensive examples from Bangla text, and the printers in England had no Bengali type. In fact, Bengali typeface had not even been created. *Code of Gentoo Laws* did have a page of Bengali letters, but for that the printers had used a block printed page of Bengali alphabet. It was not possible to print the grammar book without Bengali movable types.

K.S. Diehl notes in her essay 'Bengali Types and Their Founders' that Halhed had earlier tried to have Bengali types cast in the foundries (factories in which metal castings are produced) of England and had contacted Wilhelm Bolts, an Englishman of German origin, for this purpose. But the results were not satisfactory. Warren Hastings came to the rescue once more and prevailed upon Charles Wilkins to take on the job. Wilkins, who had arrived in India a couple of years before Halhed, and had a background in printing, willingly took on the task of preparing a set of Bengali types.

Wilkins was assisted by Panchanan Karmakar, a local punch cutter whose job was to cut letter punches in steel for making metal type. Panchanan was also a foundry operator and succeeded in developing the Bangla type for printing. His success was beyond expectation. Bangla letters appeared in print for the first time in 1778 and a Bengali press was set up at Hooghly. Thus, Halhed's *Grammar of the Bengal Language*, published in 1778, became the very first typeset book to be printed with the types of Bangla alphabet.

However, another Bengali grammar (actually dictionary-cum-grammar) had been published in Lisbon in 1743. Written by Manoel da Assumpção, a Portuguese missionary, the book was titled *Vocabulario em idioma bengalla e portugueza* (*Vocabulary of Bengali language and Portuguese*). It was written in Portuguese and used Latin script for writing Bengali words. Because of these reasons, Assumpção's book was practically unknown in Britain and Bengal. Therefore, it was Halhed's book that was hailed as the first grammar of Bengali language, and its lasting contribution to the history of Bengali culture was widely acknowledged.

Hastings was so excited by the book that in June 1778, even before the printing was completed, he presented specimen copies of the Bengali Grammar to the Council, recommending financial assistance. On the governor-general's recommendation, the book was accepted as the property of the Company. Rocher mentions in *Orientalism, Poetry, and the Millennium* that 'a gratuity (was) allowed to those gentlemen of 30 Rupees for each copy and...recommended to them to prosecute the work under the sanction and protection of this Government.'

In five years, Halhed had achieved more than many accomplish in a lifetime. Unfortunately, Halhed's glory was short-lived. His life after the publication of the grammar proved to be one debacle after another, till at last he simply faded away. Where did Halhed go wrong? A look at Halhed's life after his return to England sheds some light on the combination of factors that caused his downfall.

Some commentators feel that Halhed hitching his wagon to Warren Hastings and his influence led to him being too dependent on Hastings's favour. In 1785, after Halhed had returned to England, Hastings's policies and actions were coming in for bitter censure from his critics in England. Halhed jumped into the fray and began taking part in East India House debates. He also kept Hastings informed of the proceedings in the Parliament, primarily about the attempts being made to recall Hastings to initiate charges for crimes and misdemeanors during his time in India, especially for embezzlement, extortion and other offences. The case dragged on for seven years.

Halhed's career was now irrevocably tied up with that of Warren Hastings. He was identified as one of the chief associates of the 'Bengal Squad', which referred to the group of influential Company officials who had returned to Great Britain and had become members of the Parliament. Some historians also refer to the supporters of Hastings (Halhed being one of them), as the 'Hastings Squad'.

In 1784, financial problems forced Halhed to return to India. By then, Bengal had undergone a drastic change. Hastings had fallen completely out of favour with the Court of Directors and was dealing with persistent opposition to his policies. In the end, things became so bad for Hastings that he resigned in December 1784 and returned to England the following June. Hastings had made some powerful enemies at home and anticipated that things were likely to get much worse. With that in mind, he persuaded his supporters in India to return with him. Thus Halhed, along with the others of the 'squad', followed his mentor to England.

After returning to England, Halhed became more and more involved in the war of pamphlets (supporting his mentor Hastings against his detractors, as well as on other issues) and no longer had any time for literary activities. In 1779, he wrote an anonymous piece justifying the act by Hasting that had led to the Maratha War. Then, on 8 June 1782, he wrote a verse in an imitation of Horace's *Ode in Praise of Augustus* in which he expressed his loyalty and admiration for his mentor. Halhed also wrote a series of open letters between October 1782 and November 1783, all in defence of Hastings. These articles appeared in the daily papers as well as in separate pamphlets under the pseudonym 'Detector'.

However, he did revert, very briefly, to his original passion for oriental translations. His main literary works during this phase were translations of Hindu religious books such as the *Upanisad* (translated in 1787), which was based on Dara Shikoh's Persian translation. He also began translating the Mahabharata into English from Persian. Halhed, who had been fascinated with the Mahabharata, bemoaned the fact that he did not know enough Sanskrit to read it in the original. Unfortunately, the translation was never completed. The unfinished translation of Halhed's Mahabharata is now housed in the library of the Asiatic Society of Bengal.

The impeachment and trial of Warren Hastings began in 1787. Edmund Burke had levelled 22 charges against Hastings, who now faced impeachment on the grounds of 'high crimes and misdemeanours'. The noose was tightening around Hastings. Halhed was so deeply affected by these events that he gave up his literary studies in favour of politics and decided on a Parliamentary career. He was elected

Member of Parliament for Lymington, Hampshire for a term from 1791 to 1796.

The case against Hastings dragged on till 1795. Even though eventually Hastings was acquitted of all charges, this period marked the beginning of the downward slide in Halhed's life and career. From that point onwards, there was a total change in Halhed's focus. Scholarly pursuits were replaced with political articles and pamphlets in support of Hastings's policies.

Halhed had wanted to help Hastings, but ended up getting deeply enmeshed himself. He not only lost his money and reputation but also became an object of ridicule, being referred to as a returned nabob, an agent of an Indian prince, and a 'Hastings' man'. Next in the series of unfortunate events that came to define the latter half of Halhed's life came his ill-timed encounter with Richard Brothers.

According to the article on Halhed in *The History of Parliament Online*, Richard Brothers was a self-proclaimed apostle of a new religion who claimed to be the 'Nephew of the Almighty'. He declared himself the 'Prince of the Hebrews', who was destined to lead the Jews and rule over Israel until the return of Jesus Christ. We know from Halhed's own admission that life for him changed forever on 5 January 1795 after he read Brothers's prophecies, published as *A Revealed Knowledge of the Prophecies and Time.*

What seems totally inexplicable is the fact that someone as intelligent and clearsighted as Halhed could come under the spell of such a person. Indeed, he was so taken up by the so-called celebrant that not only did Halhed take up the task of publicizing Brothers's book but also wrote and distributed a *Testimony of the Authenticity of the Prophecies of Richard Brothers, and of his Mission to recall the Jews.* This caused an immediate and universal outcry amongst the English public, and it was generally felt that Halhed's writing were inflammatory and the outpourings of a mad and eccentric mind. Matters came to a head when Brothers was expelled from Parliament after he arrived to warn the House that the seventh chapter of the Book of Daniel was about to be fulfilled!

In 1795, Brothers was arrested and imprisoned as a criminal lunatic on charges of treason after he prophesied the death of the king and the end of the monarchy! But Halhed kept stubbornly insisting on Brothers's innocence and petitioned for him in Parliament. His credibility took another beating when he began distributing papers in the House alleging that Brothers had been prejudged a lunatic. Quoted in the previous article, George Canning, a British Tory statesman, called it 'altogether one of the most extraordinary performances that was ever heard in Parliament…' Halhed somehow managed to have the case brought before the Parliament and have Brothers removed to a private asylum.

Though Halhed eventually realized the futility of his actions and tried to make amends, it was too late. He had seriously embarrassed himself, and his reputation was in ruins. It was now clear to everyone that his political fate had been sealed. By 1796, Halhed was out of Parliament.

Things became worse when, as a demonstration of his support of the French Revolution, he transferred his lifelong savings to France for a safer and more lucrative investment. It was an unwise move, and Halhed lost a great deal of money in French *assignats* (the paper bill issued in *France* as currency during the French Revolution).

By the end of the century, Halhed was in dire financial straits and had to sell off his precious personal collection of oriental manuscripts in order to pay off his debts. He also disposed of his own unpublished works. Indeed, his situation had become so pathetic that when Mrs Hastings expressed her wish to meet him during a visit to London, he had to refuse because he did not have proper clothes for the occasion!

Halhed now desperately needed a job, and when he came to know that the Company had expanded its examiner's department and required more staff, he decided to reapply. He was hired in 1809 as chief assistant of examiner of correspondence in India House, a post with a decent salary.

One of the perks of the job was accessibility to the Company library. At the library, he discovered a handwritten manuscript by Tipu Sultan, the ruler of Mysore whose reign lasted from 1782 to 1799. It was titled *Tipu Sultan's Dreams*. Halhed was motivated to translate it into English. However, along with other translation work he did after his return from India, it didn't earn him any credit.

All his tribulations did not shake Halhed's loyalty for Hastings. In fact, his bond with the former governor-general had become even stronger, and he continued to write on issues concerning his mentor. Hastings was now almost 80 years old, and his health had failed considerably following his long trial on the mismanagement and personal corruption during his time as the first governor-general of Bengal. Halhed felt vindicated when, in June 1813, the University of Oxford conferred upon Hastings an honorary degree and, in 1814, honoured him further by making him a privy councillor.

However, this happy phase in Halhed's life was not destined to last and came to an end with Hastings's death four years later, on 22 August 1818. It left Halhed bereft. It had been the support of his mentor that had kept him afloat during the worst of times, but with the death of Hastings the last spark of creativity in him was extinguished. Unable to express his feeling in words, Halhed articulated his sentiments through two poems. He was also given the responsibility of composing the epitaph.

After this, Halhed became a total recluse and his writing activity came to a complete stop. In the spring of 1819, he resigned from the Company's services, and started to live off a pension of £500. And even though he lived for another decade, he made no attempt to write again. He was all but forgotten by the world. Thomas Moore, who had been trying to trace him for his biography of Sheridan, assumed that Halhed was dead or 'if living, in a state of wretched mental imbecility', according to the article on Halhed in *The History of Parliament Online*.

Friendless and impoverished, Nathaniel Brassey Halhed passed away on 18 February 1830 and was buried in the family grave of Petersham Parish Church.

Regardless of all the criticism heaped on Halhed's *Code of Gentoo Laws*, it remains amongst the very first attempts to codify Hindu laws in English and make the ancient Indian legal system comprehensible for British administrators. But a far more significant contribution was his assertion that Sanskrit was related to other classical languages of the world. In Halhed's preface of the Bengali grammar, we find the earliest references to the existence of the Indo-European language family.

In a letter to George Costard, quoted in Rocher's *Orientalism, Poetry, and the Millennium,* Halhed wrote that Sanskrit contained

> [E]very part of speech and every distinction which is to be found in either Greek or Latin and in some particular it is more copious than either... I do not attempt to ascertain as a fact, that either Greek or Latin are derived from this language; but I give a few reasons wherein such a conjecture might be founded: and I am sure it has a better claim to the honour of a parent than, Phoenician or Hebrew.

In the preface to his Bengali Grammar Halhed expresses his admiration, verging on veneration, of Sanskrit, which he described as 'the grand source of Indian literature, the parent of almost every dialect from the Persian Gulf to the China seas is the Shanscrit, a language of the most venerable and unfathomable antiquity...'

With regard to Halhed's remarks in the same preface about the similarity between Persian and Arabic to Latin and Greek, Professor Franklin, in his previously mentioned essay, says, 'Halhed's theory regarding the relationship of Sanskrit to other classical languages anticipates Jones' famous Third Anniversary Discourse of 1786'.

Besides correlating Sanskrit to other classical languages of Europe, Halhed was the first person to discover the connection between Indian languages and Sanskrit. Today even a child knows that Indian languages have their roots in Sanskrit; but it was Halhed who first recognized the fact that the 'Hindostanic' dialect spoken over most of 'Hindostan' was 'indubitably derived from Shanscrit', with which it had the same connection as modern dialects of France and Italy have with pure Latin, as recorded by Bernard Cohn in his 1996 book *Colonialism and its Forms of Knowledge*. He also established the relation of Bengali to Sanskrit. In his preface he wrote that 'Bengal language' was a 'derivative from its parent Shanscrit'. This makes Halhed one of the earliest persons to establish the affinity between Sanskrit and some of the Afro-Asiatic languages as well as the Indo-European language family.

Thus, Halhed has secured his place in history as one of the pioneers of modern philology. And even though he never really learnt enough Sanskrit to read the classics in the original script, he paved the ground for eminent Sanskritists like Jones and Wilkins, and prepared the way for the first great Sanskrit scholar in Europe, Henry Thomas Colebrooke.

4

JAMES PRINSEP

Decoding India's Past

'He (James Prinsep) is one of the greatest geniuses ever born, a Briton who not only documented the history of Benares in his drawings and diaries, but also deciphered two of India's ancient scripts, Brahmi and Kharoshthi. He laid the underground drainage of Benares and built the bridge over the Karmanasa River. How much can a man achieve in 10 years?'

– A.P.J. Abdul Kalam, former President of India,
in his tribute to James Prinsep[1]

1830

ONE WINTER AFTERNOON, A YOUNG ENGLISHMAN OF PREPOSSESSING appearance was seen sitting by one of the ghats in Benares (now Varanasi), on the banks of the holy river Ganges. As the sun began to set, he watched in utter fascination as life flowed along in the city. He had beside him a couple of drawing boards and a box of pencils.

---

[1] 'A tribute to the founder of modern Varanasi - James Prinsep', *TwoCircles.net*, 9 September 2009.

The air was suddenly charged with 'the music and bells of a hundred temples' and the sound struck his ear as a 'magic melody from the distance, amidst the buzz of human voices', in the Englishman's own words published in *Benares Illustrated* in 1830. That was the moment the young Englishman had been waiting for, as for him there were few objects more lively and exhilarating than the sunset hour on the banks of the Ganges. With a contented sigh, he picked up his drawing board and pencil and began to recreate the scene on paper.

That sombre young man was James Prinsep, the assay master of Benares Mint. His love for the holy city bordered on reverence. He had made the city his own.

Mark Twain, who visited India more than half a century later, expressed very similar emotions when he wrote in his 1897 book *Following the Equator* that, 'Benares is older than history, older than tradition, older even than legend and looks twice as old as all of them put together.'

James Prinsep's mind went back to the day when he had first arrived at Benares from Calcutta in 1820. He was 21 when he made that journey in a large, slow-moving boat, that the locals called *bajra*, sailing upriver for a distance of almost 700 miles. He had travelled for more than a week before he got his first glimpse of Benares. And, from that moment, the city had taken a mesmeric hold over him.

His very first impression of the city is recorded in a letter to his father. As recorded by Charles Allen in his book *The Buddha and the Sahibs* published in 2015, Prinsep describes Benares as 'a real town, extensive and of stone... the ghats on the banks of the sacred Ganges are really superb.' He was so overwhelmed that he felt that words were inadequate to do justice to the city. Instead, he wrote to his father that he would rather make a few sketches 'which would do much more in the way of description than all I could say.'

James continued making extensive pencil-and-ink drawings and engravings during his ten years in Benares. He tried to capture every aspect of the sacred city: the ancient buildings, the temples, the mosques and minarets, as well as the dancers, the musicians, the bazaars, and, of course, the ghats, crowded with pilgrims performing their holy rituals.

These sketches were not just the doodles of an amateur; James was a talented artist. A collection of seventeen of his drawings was published in 1831 under the title *Benares Illustrated.* This book introduced Benares to the Western world and made this holy city of India famous. Soon after in 1833, another volume with a few additional drawings was published.

James contributed a lot more to the city than just his paintings. He undertook, with tremendous zeal, a large number of projects that affected the lives of the residents of Benares. According to the historian and writer O.P. Kejariwal's *The Asiatic Society of Bengal and the Discovery of India's Past* published in 1988, Prinsep contributed more to this holy city than any individual in Indian history. A look at James Prinsep's early life gives us an idea of how the versatility and skills he acquired in his childhood blossomed after he came to India in 1819.

James Prinsep was born to John Prinsep and Sophia Elizabeth Auriol on 20 August 1799 in Chelsea, a county in Essex, England. James was the tenth child, and the seventh son, of his parents. He was unusually brilliant right from his childhood, demonstrating not only a flair for drawing and music but also outstanding dexterity in science. By the time he was 15, he was displaying consummate skill in multiple disciplines.

Like many other Englishmen those days, John decided to leave for India in search of fortune in 1771. A canny businessman, John realized the lucrative potential of indigo cultivation early on, and set himself up as a commercial indigo planter. The major factor that helped John succeed was his acquaintance with Warren Hastings, who was the governor-general of India at the time. John used Hastings's influence to get a monopoly on the lucrative trade. For a while, John was one of the richest men in Calcutta. He returned to England, having amassed a fortune of £40,000 and established himself as an East India merchant.

Back in England, he tried to continue his business but unfortunately for him, he faced a reversal of fortune and lost most of his wealth. As a result, John moved with his family to Clifton in 1809. Initially, James and his two younger brothers, Thomas and Augustus, were sent to study in a school in Clifton run by a Mr Bullock. The two years he studied in this school was to be the only formal education James would ever receive.

However, James had a tremendous thirst for knowledge and learnt a lot more at home on his own initiative, with help from his older siblings. From his sisters, he acquired a taste in music. When he was 15, his father decided that it was time for James to prepare for his future vocation. Keeping in mind his son's ingenuity and skill in design, he felt that he was best suited for a career in architecture. So, he sent James to study with Augustus Pugin, a renowned architect of the time. But an eye injury changed the course of his life.

Fortunately, John had been astute enough to maintain his old connections with India and used his sources to get information about a possible future opening in the assay department of the Calcutta Mint. He sent James to be apprenticed with a Mr Bingley, the assay master of the Royal Mint of London. James received a certificate of proficiency after the completion of a one-year assistantship. This training was to help him obtain his first job in India.

In early 1819, he received an appointment as assistant to the assay master of the Calcutta Mint. At the age of 20, James set sail for India, with his younger brother Thomas who secured an appointment with the Bengal Engineers. The latter had secured employment in the East India Company army. They journeyed aboard a ship named *Hooghly,* and landed at Chandpal Ghat in Calcutta on the morning of 15 September 1819, according to the *Dictionary of National Biography.* They were received by their brother Henry Thoby, who was a civil servant in Calcutta.

Since James had been deprived of a formal education, his career in India began in the fairly modest position of assistant assay master. However, he would go on to work under Dr Horace Hayman Wilson, a Sanskrit scholar who was the honorary secretary to the Asiatic Society of Bengal and one of the most eminent oriental scholars of the time. It was under Wilson that James's love for ancient Indian literature and history was nourished. But at first, James would find the meetings of the Asiatic Society quite boring and wrote to his father that the meetings always made him sleepy.

Wilson was sent to Benares by Hastings to remodel the mint there. His replacement in Calcutta was a Dr Atkinson, a gentleman who was more concerned with safeguarding his own position than his work. As a result, most of the workload was transferred to James and he ended up performing all the duties of the assay master. However, this proved to be a blessing in disguise for James, as he soon became adept in the process of assaying and other related technical details.

Wilson returned to Calcutta in April 1821, and James Prinsep was appointed assay master of the Benares Mint, where he worked from 1820–30. Prinsep left for Benares a month later, hiring another boat to carry scientific equipment, books and papers that he had collected in the hope of setting up a science laboratory. This posting proved to be the defining moment in Prinsep's life and brought to fruition all of his scientific and architectural knowledge. It would help him lay the foundation of modern Varanasi. According to Kejariwal, 'during the 10 years that Prinsep stayed in Varanasi, he identified himself with the city so much that he came to be known as Benares Prinsep'.

Prinsep's contribution to the country is so extensive that it is difficult to summarize it in a few pages. His life and work in India can be divided into three distinct phases. First, the Benares phase, which sees the culmination of his artistic and engineering skills. Second, the literary phase, which begins after his return to Calcutta. In this phase, he wrote extensively on a wide variety of topics related to Indian antiquities. In the third, and most significant phase, Prinsep's attention shifted to numismatics and epigraphs. During this period, he was completely focused on decoding the early inscriptions which ultimately resulted in the reconstruction of India's history preceding the advent of the Muslims.

'Benares, A Brahmin placing a garland on the holiest spot in the sacred city', taken from James Prinsep's *Benares Illustrated*.

Prinsep's first task at the Benares Mint was the reconstruction of the building the mint was housed in. By the time he arrived in Benares, the foundation of the new mint had already been laid, and a portion of the structure had been erected; however, Prinsep was dissatisfied with the design. Since the building was to be his office-cum-residence, he submitted an amended plan to the military board at Calcutta, and undertook the job without any increase in the estimated cost of the original design.

The construction of this building brought to light Prinsep's great architectural talent. It led to him being commissioned for several new works in the city, including the reconstruction of the minarets of Aurangzeb. He also took on the renovation of the St. Mary's Church and the Nandeswar Kothi (a palace of the Benares royalty).

To Prinsep also goes the credit of drawing up the first detailed map of Benares that showed every building in the city. It was a complex and laborious task that took him two years to complete. In a letter to his father quoted by Allen, Prinsep described the project as 'a stupendous work of labour a stupendous work of labour...a work never yet undertaken'. Elegantly illustrated copies of the map were sent to the colonial government and other authorities. In the same letter, he mentions another map to be made in 'Nagri (Devanagari) for the benefit of the Hindoos'. Amongst the other projects initiated by Prinsep during this time was the first census of Benares and the preparation of the first directory of the city.

One of the factors that worked in Prinsep's favour was the timing of his arrival. He came to India almost 25 years after William Jones's death, and by that time the political situation in India had changed drastically. The British were now undisputed masters of the country. By 1823, the colonial government was in a position to allocate large sums of money for the improvement of major cities and allowed public officers to apply for the funds as required. It was around this time that Prinsep was appointed a member and secretary of the Benares committee, which placed him in a position to fulfil his projects without any hindrance.

Prinsep's next important undertaking was the building of a deep underground tunnel for draining a swamp in the lowest part of Benares. He was engaged in this work for two years. Though in some places the tunnel was dug under buildings and homes, no accident was reported. He followed this up with the successful renovation and restoration of several other permanent structures.

Yet another engineering triumph was the construction of a stone bridge over the river Karmanasa, a tributary of the Ganges that separates Uttar Pradesh from Bihar. It was a difficult task that had discouraged engineers and architects until then. 'Karmanasa' literally means 'destroyer of merit'. The river was named so because it was believed to be cursed.

There was a superstition among the locals that if a returning pilgrim's feet got wet by the river's waters, it would wash away the merit they had gained by bathing in the Ganges. Because of this belief, it became customary for Hindus to cross one of the shallower parts of the river riding on the back of a brahmin. The brahmins did not mind this arrangement as it was very lucrative for them – they charged the pilgrims a huge amount of money for carrying them. No wonder then that the construction of a bridge over the

Karmanasa was not in their interest, and they declared the task impossible.

However, when construction of the bridge was mooted by Prinsep, the governor-general readily agreed as it was for a good cause. Prinsep's persuasive powers garnered the popular support of the people and overcame the resistance of the priests. Soon work began. The cost of building this 'substantial stone bridge of three arches' was more than 6 lakh rupees, and was covered by a rich merchant and philanthropist of Benares by the name of Patni Mal, according to Allen's book.

Allen further mentions that on the completion of the bridge, James's elder brother William observed proudly: 'What better monument to his (James's) memory could he have than the blessing of every Hindoo walking dry footed across this accursed stream.'

It was in Benares that Prinsep's talent for science got wings. He made every effort to keep pace with the progress of science in Europe. Such was his zeal for scientific studies that even while he was conducting major engineering projects, he was simultaneously carrying out several scientific experiments on the side. Prinsep made regular meteorological observations and also invented a pyrometer. His paper 'On the Measurement of High Temperature' was published in the Royal Society's journal called 'Philosophical Transactions' and earned him the position of a Fellow of the Royal Society.

Besides this, volume three of *The Quarterly Oriental Magazine, Review, and Register* mentions that he developed a pluviometer (for measuring rain) and an evaporimeter (for determining the extent of evaporation). He was equally skilled at mechanics, and made a balance of such accuracy that it could indicate the three-thousandth part of a grain in assay operations. On his departure, the colonial government purchased his balance for use in the Calcutta Mint.

During the period he was immersed in scientific activities, Prinsep was also in touch with the academic circle of Calcutta where several of his papers were published. He was in constant communication with the Asiatic Society, of which he was elected a member in 1830. Prinsep formed a literary society called Benares Literary Society in 1822 in partnership with A. Duvancel, a French naturalist, and set up a press for printing the proceedings of this society.

Prinsep's image as a renaissance man would be incomplete if we were to leave out one of the lesser-known aspects of his personality: his great fondness for music and plays. In fact, he regularly participated in musical soirées and acted in plays. H.E. Cotton mentions in his 1950 book *Calcutta, Old and New* that a distinguished French botanist and a celebrated traveller by the name of Victor Jacquemont was in Benares in 1830, and he recorded that, 'James devotes his mornings to architectural plans and drawings, his days at the Mint and his evenings to musical concerts.'

Prinsep's sojourn in Benares came to an end with the abolishment of the Benares Mint in 1830. He was recalled to Calcutta and appointed deputy assay master under his old supervisor, Dr Horace Hayman Wilson. But Prinsep's hopes to become the assay master of the Calcutta Mint were dashed when it was officially announced that Dr Atkinson would be succeeding Wilson. However, as fate would have it, Atkinson was found to be involved in a financial fraud, resulting in his removal from office by the new Governor-General Lord Bentinck.

Prinsep marked his return to Calcutta with an engineering achievement – the excavation of the canal that connected the Hooghly with the Sunderbans. The canal was important for providing additional passage for the increasing traffic between Calcutta and the eastern districts of Bengal. Originally, the task of linking the canals (collectively known as Eastern Canals) was being handled by James's brother Thomas, who was superintendent of canals.

However, before the project could be completed, Thomas died after falling from his horse. James decided to take over from where his brother had left off, and completed it to the satisfaction of the authorities. According to the Prinsep brothers' *Essays on Indian Antiquities: Historic, Numismatic, and Palæographic* published in 1858, 'The locks, built by him in the midst of a soil of quicksand, upon a principle of his own devising, were regarded as a highly skilful piece of engineering.'

Prinsep's literary interests came to the fore in Calcutta. His literary phase began in 1831 when he started a paper named 'Gleanings in Science' in partnership with Major Herbert, an officer of the Company's army. Prinsep contributed extensively to this paper. However, Herbert had to leave for England before the year was out and Prinsep took over the running of this periodical.

He decided to re-model the journal and *Asiatic Researches* was merged with 'Gleanings' and renamed as the 'Journal of the Asiatic Society of Bengal'. Prinsep was not just the editor and publisher for the journal but also the engraver and lithographer. His plan was to compile and publish it on a monthly basis and, at the end of the year, bring out a bound volume of all twelve issues published that year. The first bound volume of the 'Journal of the Asiatic Society of Bengal' appeared in 1832.

In the same year, Prinsep's mentor Wilson left for England after his appointment as the first Boden Professor of Sanskrit at Oxford. This position was established in the University of Oxford in 1832 with money donated to the university by Lieutenant Colonel Joseph Boden, a retired soldier in the service of the East India Company. His aim was to establish a Sanskrit professorship to assist in the conversion of the people of British India to Christianity, and his bequest was also used to fund scholarships in Sanskrit at Oxford.

Therefore, Prinsep succeeded Wilson as the assay master at the Calcutta Mint. He was also appointed secretary of the Asiatic Society. In this latter role, Prinsep began to follow in the wake of Jones, Colebrooke and Wilson in the field of Indian antiquities.

The 'Journal of the Asiatic Society of Bengal', Vol. 1 (January to December 1832), edited by James Prinsep, begins with a quote from William Jones: 'it will flourish, if naturalists, chemists, antiquaries, philologers, and men of science, in different parts of Asia will commit their observations to writing, and send them to the Asiatic Society, in Calcutta...' It gives a clear indication that Prinsep was trying to broaden the scope of the journal. Like Jones, Prinsep aimed to widen the range of the society's studies by inviting contributions from 'all those who cultivated scientific or literary pursuits connected with the East.'

Prinsep contributed a number of valuable articles on diverse subjects such as chemistry, mineralogy, Indian numismatics and Indian antiquities. In the process, he succeeded in infusing new life into oriental studies. Under Prinsep's inspiration, the Society started to receive archaeological material as well. Not since the time of William Jones had the Asiatic Society of Bengal seen so much activity.

Prinsep reached the apogee of his career in the period from 1833 to 1838. After groundbreaking work in the field of science, architecture and statistics, he moved to the third phase of his career. It was at the time that he turned his attention to discovering India's early history. With no recorded history to help him, Prinsep focused his attention on the study of numismatics, epigraphs and ancient archaeological ruins to discover India's past.

Within six years, he was able to accomplish the seemingly impossible task of lifting the veil from India's hidden past. History was reconstructed and the names of some of the most important ruling dynasties of ancient India were revealed. Of the numerous contributions made by Prinsep, if we were to choose just one that gives him a permanent place in Indian history, it would be the decoding of India's past through scientific archaeology.

From time immemorial, scholars had been mystified by the numerous inscriptions carved on ancient monuments and rocks scattered all over the country. Despite many attempts to make sense of these writings, researchers had failed in deciphering the ancient writing system. Ultimately, it was Prinsep who decoded the long-forgotten scripts of Brahmi and Kharoshti, in which many of these early inscriptions were written.

The earliest recorded attempt at understanding the writings was made in the fourteenth century CE, during the reign of Sultan Firoz Shah (1351-1388). The story goes that Firoz Shah came upon two inscribed Ashokan pillars during one of his campaigns. One pillar was at Topra near Ambala and the other near Meerut. Enthralled by the magnificent pillars, he decided to have them carried all the way to Delhi.

The Delhi Information website describes that the pillars were carefully wrapped with cotton silk and 'transported on a massive carriage attached with 42 wheels and drawn meticulously by 200 men from their original places to Delhi.... Upon reaching Delhi, they were then transported on huge boats to their final destination.' It is said he employed brahmin scholars to read the engravings but the attempts to decipher the writing on the pillar failed.

For the next 200 years, there was no mention of the pillars. It was as if they had been forgotten. The next time they cropped up was in 1616, when an English traveller by the name of Thomas Coryat happened to notice one in the ruins of Firozabad, now Firoz Shah Kotla. It was about 40 feet high, and in the evening light it appeared, from a distance, to be made of brass. When Coryat got closer, he thought it was made of marble, but it was only when he was within touching distance of the pillar did he realize that it was sandstone, polished to a mirror finish.

Coryat noticed that there were two main inscriptions on the pillar. He was particularly fascinated by one of the scripts, which consisted of simple erect letters that appeared to him to be a bit like pin-men or stick figures. He assumed that the lettering was Greek and that the pillar commemorated Alexander's invasion of India. And there the matter rested.

About half a century later, an East India Company employee named John Marshall (not to be confused with John Hubert Marshall, who served as the director-general of archaeology in India) was posted to Singhiya in Bihar. There, he heard about a strange pillar located approximately 20 miles north of the town. According to local legends, the pillar was the *gada,* or club, of Bhima, the second of the five Pandava brothers from the Mahabharata. According to the epic, Bhima was of gigantic proportions and used that staff to grind his *bhang* (an edible preparation of cannabis).

Marshall's curiosity was aroused, and he went on an expedition to this remote area. In a journal entry by him dated 30 July 1670, and quoted in *John Marshall in India: Notes and Observations in Bengal, 1668-1672* from 1927, he describes 'Bhima's club' as:

> a Piller (Pillar) of one stone as I conceive. It is 9 yards 9 inches high and 3 yards 33 inches thick or round about. At the top of this pillar or Lattee (lathi, staff, club) is placed a Tyger (lion actually) ingraven, the neatliest that I have seen in India...

The discovery of this pillar, similar to the one in Firoz Shah Kotla but situated hundreds of miles away, put paid to Coryat's theory that these were of Greek origin. Alexander is not considered to have been to Delhi nor Bihar, which further debunked any theory of these inscriptions celebrating Alexander's conquests.

By this time, similar 'pin-men' inscriptions had been reported in caves and temples in many parts of the subcontinent. Clearly, all these monuments were somehow connected. During the next 15 years, a few more inscriptions were noticed and studied, but it was only with the arrival of Prinsep on the scene that epigraphy and palaeography attracted the serious attention of scholars.

Interestingly, one serious attempt at deciphering was made by J.H. Harington (later, the Chief Judge Sadar Diwani and Nizamat Adalat) in 1798, when he presented to the Asiatic Society the *Book of Drawings and Inscriptions.* The book, published by him and prepared under the direction of Captain James Hoare, contained copies of inscriptions on the celebrated pillars of Delhi and Allahabad. Harington noted in reference to the inscriptions taken from Firoz Shah's Lat (or pillar/lattee) that the same characters appeared in the inscription on the pillar at Allahabad. Strangely enough, the book was ignored and forgotten, and gathered dust for thirty years till Prinsep found it. He republished Harington's copies of inscriptions in the 'Journal of the Asiatic Society'.

More than 35 years later, an antiquarian by the name of T.S. Burt made a detailed drawing of the Allahabad pillar. He painstakingly copied the inscriptions on the pillar and sent it to Prinsep, who in turn put together the drawings along with a classified table of the Ashokan letters and published it in the journal. This led to the significant discovery that the Allahabad pillar had three types of inscriptions, clearly belonging to different eras.

There were two long inscriptions, in addition to a Persian inscription of the Mughal period, running right down the middle of the pillar. Prinsep assumed that the oldest inscription was always positioned on top, followed by others that were added later. He also surmised that the archaic characters on top of the pillar were among the rarest of the epigraphs known in India.

His assumption, as we now know, was correct. The top inscription was in Ashokan Brahmi, known to be the earliest writing system after the Indus script. Not only are all the modern Indian scripts derived from Brahmi but also hundreds of other scripts found in southeast and east Asia.

It needs to be mentioned here that although both inscriptions in the middle of the pillar were Brahmi, there were a number of differences between the two. The first inscription, Ashokan Brahmi, belonged to the third century while the second inscription dated from 400 CE during the Gupta period and hence came to be known as Gupta Brahmi.

However, at this stage Prinsep erroneously believed that these were the same inscriptions as those discovered by Charles Wilkins at Gaya 50 years earlier. For further confirmation, the facsimiles were sent to Captain Troyer, a prominent Sanskrit scholar who was the secretary of Sanskrit College in Calcutta. With the help of a pandit, Troyer was able to read parts of the inscription, which revealed that the inscription had been engraved on the directives of a king called Samudragupta, the son of Chandragupta. This was the very first reference to King Samudragupta. What surprised and baffled Prinsep was the unexpected discovery that there were two Chandraguptas!

The confusion arose because of the assumption that this Chandragupta was the same king referred to by the Greek historians as Sandrocottus, and identified by Jones as belonging to the Maurya dynasty. However, this idea had to be abandoned because of several incongruities; firstly, there was no mention of a Samudragupta in Jones's list of Maurya kings; secondly, of the two Chandraguptas mentioned in the inscriptions deciphered by Prinsep, the first Chandragupta was apparently the father of Samudragupta and the other, Chandragupta II, his grandson. Another disputable fact was the location of the monument; this was located in Allahabad, while the capital of Chandragupta Maurya had already been established by Jones as located in Pataliputra (Patna).

A few months later, William Hodge Mill – a prominent Sanskrit scholar who was also the principal of Bishop's College in Shibpur, Calcutta – made an attempt to retranslate the inscription on the Allahabad pillar. Initially, Mill too worked under the hypothesis that the Chandragupta mentioned here was the same one Jones had identified. But after Prinsep understood that there were too many discrepancies between the two Chandraguptas for them to be the same person, it became easy for Mill to rework many of the names. He was then in a position to prepare a proper genealogical table of the entire Gupta dynasty. This was the very first attempt at writing Indian history based on the critical examination of sources and on authentic materials.

Prinsep then turned his attention to the study of the coins kept in the museum of the Asiatic Society. Being an expert in numismatics, Prinsep hoped to find some clues that would unlock the remaining secrets concealed within these ancient writings. He soon found that the lettering on some gold and silver coins had an uncanny resemblance to the characters used in the Lat of Firoz Shah in Delhi. This was a small step towards the final solution.

The actual breakthrough came after Prinsep was contacted by Brian Houghton Hodgson, a British resident of Kathmandu who had discovered the literature of northern Buddhism. Hodgson told Prinsep that during his travels to and from Kathmandu 8 or 10 years earlier, he had come across two inscribed pillars in Bihar: one at Lauriya Araraj and the other at Rampurva. Much excited, he had sent the details of these pillars to H.H. Wilson, the secretary of the Asiatic Society at the time. Inexplicably, Wilson had paid no heed to this discovery.

On reading Prinsep's articles in the 'Journal of the Asiatic Society', Hodgson wrote saying that he had found a third inscribed pillar: at Lauriya Nandangarh, a mile north of Rampurva. This was the only pillar with a perfect lion capital, though slightly damaged by a cannon shot. Hodgson also sent Prinsep the facsimile of the inscription on this pillar. Examining this facsimile, Prinsep found that it was Ashokan Brahmi. After making a comparative study of the writings on all three pillars, he came to the momentous conclusion that all three inscriptions were identical. Prinsep now knew without a doubt that these were all Ashokan inscriptions.

However, it was not the end of his quest, since many questions remained unanswered. He still had no clue about the message conveyed by the writings and the reasons behind erecting the pillars and incising them. Did they mark the conquests of a victorious king? Were they the boundary pillars of his dominions? Or were they of a religious nature? The riddle could only be satisfactorily solved by the discovery of the language in which these were written.

The next major step toward decipherment was taken by Christian Lassen, a Norwegian academic and a scholar of Sanskrit and Pali. Lassen had accidentally come upon a bilingual coin belonging to the second century BCE. He was amazed when he noticed that the legend on the coins resembled some of the characters in the pillar inscriptions, and promptly brought the matter to Prinsep's notice.

It was now clear that the coin belonged to the Indo-Greek king Agathocles, as it displayed the Greek legend *Basileos Agathokleous* on the obverse side. Lassen guessed that the reverse legend would be in an Indian dialect that was a translation of the Greek inscription. He read the reverse legend from left to right as 'Agathakula Raja', which was very close to the correct translation. This reading led to the identification of the inscription. It also became clear that the language, though Indian, was not Sanskrit. According to the Society's journal, the inscriptions deciphered in 1838 were in the Brahmi and Kharosthi scripts. These were written in Pali and Prakrit language.

Prinsep was excited by this discovery, but he was still far from the final solution. Every morning for seven years, he spread before him the facsimiles of the inscriptions collected from different parts of India and wistfully gazed at the unknown alphabets that concealed the mystery of India's past. The most significant input after this came from Captain Edward Smith, who had been drawing and copying the numerous short votive records on the famous stupa at Sanchi. Ultimately, it was the reproduction of these inscriptions that gave Prinsep the key to unlock the riddle of the long-forgotten script.

Prinsep had spent days arranging and lithographing the numerous scraps of facsimiles of the Sanchi inscriptions that had been sent to him by Captain Smith. One day, Prinsep became aware that all of them terminated with the same two letters: 𑀤𑀸 𑀦𑀁. The fact that these inscriptions were extremely brief and positioned apart from each other led him to conclude that they were records of either obituary notices, or, in his own words from volume 6 of the 'Journal of the Asiatic Society' published in 1837, 'more probably the offerings and presents of votaries, as is known to be the present custom in the Buddhist temples of Ava (Burmese/Myanmar kingdom)…' Prinsep guessed that each brief sentence had to be 'Of so and so the gift'. This led to the recognition of the word *danam* (gift). The identification of the word also taught him (in his own words) 'the very two letters, d and n, most different from the known forms, and which had foiled me most in my former attempts.' Prinsep was ecstatic; 'In the course of a few minutes,' he wrote, 'I thus became possessed of the whole alphabet, which I tested by applying it to the inscription on the Delhi column'.

Following his decipherment of the Brahmi script in 1837, Prinsep was able to partially read the opening part of the inscription on Firoz Shah's Lat, and by corroborating it with his reading of the Girnar inscriptions, he was able to give a correct reading as *Devanampiya piyadasi raja hevam aha* (Thus speaks King Piyadasi, beloved of the gods). No doubt it was a triumph; but to Prinsep it was just a partial victory because an important question still remained unanswered: who was Piyadasi?

Prinsep was bewildered. He wrote, 'in all the Hindu genealogical tables with which I am acquainted, no prince can be discovered possessing this very remarkable name.' Initially, he identified *Devanampiya* with the Sri Lankan king Devenipeatissa (mentioned in *Mahavamsa*), who had introduced Buddhism in Sri Lanka. However, with help from a famous Pali scholar from the Ceylon civil service by the name of George Turnour, Prinsep was able to eventually name the monarch. The identification was based on the authority of *Dipavamsa* (The Chronicle of the Island), the oldest historical record of Sri Lanka, which refers to the grandson of Chandragupta, and son of Bindusara, as Piyadasi. It was now proved beyond doubt that King Piyadasi mentioned in the inscriptions was no other than King Ashoka!

This was a defining moment in Prinsep's life. Famous historian D.R. Bhandarkar wrote, as quoted in the 1939 book *Revealing India's Past* edited by John Cumming: 'How exceedingly proud must the Indologists be of James Prinsep, who without such extraneous aid, unravelled the value of the larger portion of the Brahmi alphabet in which the famous edicts of the Maurya Emperor, Ashoka, and the well-known coins of Western Kshatrapas were engraved.'

Unlike many of his countrymen, Prinsep acknowledged a number of Indian scholars who helped him in reading and translating the inscriptions, including Ratna Pala. However, he reserves special praise for Kamala Kanta Vidyalankara, the person most deeply involved in his project. In volume 12 of the 'Journal of the Asiatic Society of Bengal' published in 1843, he mentions Kamala Kanta's 'critical ingenuity and wonderful acumen' has also been praised by Henry Whitlock Torrens, secretary of the Asiatic Society from 1843 to 1855: 'No Pundit has exercised himself in the act of decyphering to the extent to which has Kamalakanta.'

No doubt, Prinsep had received help from many quarters but ultimately it was his ingenuity, perseverance and single-minded devotion that produced the results and led to a proper understanding of the chronology of historical sites and events.

Prinsep married rather late in life. He tied the knot with Harriet Sophia Aubert, eldest daughter of Lieutenant-Colonel Jeremiah Aubert of the Bengal army. The wedding took place in Calcutta on 25 April 1835. Unfortunately, they were not destined to enjoy conjugal bliss for long, as the relentless work and intense exertion involved in his epigraphic and scientific pursuits took a toll on Prinsep's health and impaired his brain.

Prinsep set sail for England in October 1839. A glorious phase of Indological studies ended when he eventually died of dementia on 22 April 1840. He was not even 40. The news of Prinsep's death was received with profound grief in Calcutta. A meeting was held at the Town Hall on 30 July 1840 to honour Prinsep. It was attended by 500 people who considered him their close friend. E. Ryan, the chief justice of Bengal, read the address, alluding to Prinsep's 'prepossessing appearance, extensive accomplishment and his willing gentleness, which made him the most admired and loved of what was then a very large society'.

Renowned botanist Dr Hugh Falconer had high praise for Prinsep's intellectual character. In an obituary published in the *Colonial Magazine*, and quoted from the first volume of the *Archaeological Survey of India* published in 1873, Falconer wrote:

> Prinsep's most prominent feature was enthusiasm – one of the prime elements of genius; a burning, irrepressible enthusiasm, to which nothing could set bounds. His powers of perception were impressed with genius – they were clear, vigorous and instantaneous. The extent of his capacity was wonderful, and the number and variety of his acquirements no less remarkable.

K.N. Dixit, former director-general of the Archaeological Survey of India, quoted in *The Vedic Age* published in 1951, aptly sums up the legacy of this great man:

> Prinsep's great discovery ushered in a new era by lifting the veil from the earlier Indian inscriptions and laid the foundation of research in Indian history and practically every branch of Indian archaeology. Hereafter it became possible to evaluate each discovery and assign it to its proper period.... Scholars like Fergusson, Cunningham, Dr Bhau Daji and Dr Rajendra Lal Mitra handed on the torch lighted by Prinsep and built foundations of our present knowledge of Indian architecture, Indian geography, Indian coins during the next generation.

The citizens of Calcutta united in erecting a monument in his memory. Designed by W. Fitzgerald, it was a grand Palladian porch with Greek and Gothic inlays. Named the Prinsep Ghat, it was erected on the banks of the river Hooghly. The ghat stands even today and is a top tourist attraction, and one of the oldest recreational spots of modern Kolkata.

5

THE DANIELLS

Artist-Adventurers Transcribing the Oriental Landscape

'The execution of these drawings is indeed masterly; there is every reason to confide in the fidelity of the representations; and the effect produced by this rich and splendid display of oriental scenery is truly striking. In looking at it, one may almost feel the warmth of an Indian sky, the water seems to be in actual motion and the animals, trees and plants are studies for the naturalist.'

– A tribute to the Daniells in the *Calcutta Monthly Magazine*[1]

Early 1786, Calcutta

THERE WAS MUCH EXCITEMENT WHEN THE BRITISH LANDSCAPE artists Thomas and William Daniells arrived in Calcutta. William Hickey, an English lawyer who was in Calcutta during this time, described the uncle-nephew team as 'two

---

[1] Quoted by Thomas Sutton in his book *The Daniells: Artists and Travellers*, published in 1954.

artists of splendid talents', as quoted by *Thomas Sutton in his book The Daniells: Artists and Travellers* published in 1954. Thomas Daniell, 37, and his nephew William Daniell, 17, were soon becoming a popular topic of discussion amongst the upper crust of the Calcutta society. It was being said that the newly arrived artists had begun sketching the picturesque scenes of Calcutta very soon after landing in the city.

Luckily for the Daniells, the year they arrived in India coincided with the startup of the new weekly English-language newspaper *The Calcutta Chronicle and General Advertiser*, published in Calcutta by Stuart and Cooper. The paper began publishing on January 26, 1786. According to Sutton, public curiosity was piqued a few months later when, on 17 July 1786, the following advertisement appeared in the *Calcutta Chronicle*: 'Mr Daniell proposes to publish twelve views of Calcutta, at twelve gold Mohurs the set, from complete plates and finished in watercolours. The subscription list is open till Jan 1, 1787.' In May the following year, another notice appeared in the same paper, stating that, 'Mr Daniell has completed six of the views and will deliver impressions as soon as possible.' It was further mentioned that non-subscribers would have to pay 18 gold mohurs.

A similar report was also published in the *Calcutta Gazette*, one of the first English newspapers in Bengal: 'Mr Daniell, having completed six of the plates of his views, hopes to deliver prints in the course of next month. The remainder will be delivered as finished. He begs subscribers to forward the amount of their subscription.'

Thomas had been busy drawing and sketching different views of this fascinating city. He was committed to producing

12 images representing Calcutta. It was a laborious task because, while drawing the scenery was easy, the engraving of the aquatint plates – a method of etching a printing plate so that tones similar to watercolour washes can be reproduced – was a highly complex process.

Since aquatinting was a technique which the Daniells had yet to master, they decided to employ local artists for the same. We know this because a friend of Thomas by the name of William Baillie, as quoted by Sutton in his book, mentions that, 'All Daniell's views were stained (coloured) principally by natives.'

With help from Indian craftsmen, they succeeded in completing the set. In November 1788, the 12 *Views of Calcutta* were published at 12 gold mohurs to subscribers and 18 gold mohurs to non-subscribers. *Views of Calcutta* got lavish praise from many quarters and sold well.

To really appreciate the historical importance of the Daniells' work, we need to keep in mind that although a large number of European travellers had visited India during the seventeenth and eighteenth centuries and had left accounts of their travels, there was no visual record of the country. The Daniells were the earliest British artists to portray Indian life, not in isolation but as part of the lush Indian landscape and cityscapes that included buildings, roads, transportation and monuments. They portrayed India as they saw it.

This was in sharp contrast to the other artists of the time, who were, with the exception of William Hodges, mostly portrait painters. Landscape painting had not yet caught on in India. It was more lucrative to paint portraits as portrait painters enjoyed a lot of patronage, not only of nabobs of the East India Company but also of Indian royal families. Though Hodges had earned quite a name for himself for his true-to-life delineation of Indian landscape, his progress was hindered because, like most artists of his time, he limited his area of work to certain regions and rarely ventured outside the districts administered by the East India Company.

No other European artists had travelled so widely and covered so much of India as the Daniells, and none had provided such a vibrant visual image of India based on first-hand observations. Their uniqueness lies in the fact that they succeeded in presenting to the Western world a view of India that was the closest to reality. In this chapter, we shall trace the enthralling journey of two English painters who became the most celebrated landscape artists of their time.

Thomas Daniell was born in 1749 in Kingston upon Thames to the innkeeper of the Swan Inn at Chertsey. Starting his professional career with odd jobs such as bricklaying or coach-painting, Thomas soon became an apprentice to a coachbuilder by the name of Maxwell in London. After completing his apprenticeship in 1770, he began working for Charles Catton, coach-painter to George III. This experience was to stand young Thomas in good stead, as it was the beginning of his love affair with colours.

At the age of 24, Thomas Daniell went on to study painting at The Royal Academy of Arts, in London. It was here that his artistic talent blossomed. Between 1772 and 1784, 30 of his artworks were exhibited at the academy. Initially his subjects included themes from literature, flowers, landscapes, portraits and even animals.

Unfortunately, Thomas's brother William passed away in 1779, following which he adopted his nephew, also named William. Thereby, William junior, who was also artistically inclined and highly talented, began living with his uncle and assisting him in his work. He also began to train himself in the art of aquatint, a popular technique with printmakers to achieve a tone similar to watercolour washes.

Around that time, the East was becoming a popular destination with European artists. William Hodges, Tilly Kettle, Ozias Humphrey, Johann Zoffany and others were known to have acquired both fame and riches after moving to Asia. During those days, Europeans wanting to travel to India had to get permission from the East India Company and Thomas had applied. It is interesting to note that although he was still an amateur in the art of printmaking, Thomas's application shows his profession as an 'engraver', or printmaker. He was probably aware of the dearth of engravers in the Indian presidency towns and realized that engraving would be far more lucrative for him.

Thomas's authorization to travel to Calcutta to work as an engraver arrived in December 1784, and soon after, he received permission to take William with him as an assistant. On 7 April 1785, Thomas and William Daniell boarded *Atlas,* a well-known merchant ship of the time, and set sail for India via China.

They arrived at Whampoa in China on 23 August, took a country ship to Calcutta from there and reached their destination in early 1786. Their perception of the city was based on what they had read about it. Calcutta, the capital of British India, had been described by a french army officer, Louis de Grandpré in his 1803 book *A Voyage in the Indian Ocean and to Bengal*, as 'not only the handsomest town in Asia but one of the finest in the world'. And indeed, the city left the Daniells spellbound.

Soon after their arrival in Calcutta, the duo set to work and became engrossed in sketching the beautiful garden houses, the wide roads with imposing European-style buildings, the bustling riverside, the crowded ghats, the grain bazaar and other sights of the city. While painting, they also took up odd jobs to sustain themselves.

At that time, the old court house of Calcutta was being shifted to a new venue. Thomas and William undertook the task of removing the paintings that adorned the old building and hanging them in the new courthouse after cleaning and repairing. They also painted portraits of rich patrons to supplement their income.

They finally completed their 12 paintings in November 1788 and began creating a set of coloured aquatints titled *Views of Calcutta*. It had taken them 12 months to complete the 12 *Views of Calcutta,* and the project left Thomas absolutely depleted. He wrote to his friend Ozias Humphry, a well-known painter of portrait miniatures, as recorded by Sutton: 'The Lord be praised, at length, I have completed my 12 views of Calcutta. The fatigue I have experienced... has almost worn me out.'

According to contemporary reports the paintings proved to be extraordinarily popular among both Indian and European clients. However, despite the accolades from the public, Thomas himself was not too happy with the outcome.

Sutton mentions that their patron William Hickey too felt that 'being the first attempt they proved very inferior to many subsequent performances.' The subsequent work Hickey was referring to no doubt is *Oriental Scenery*, the Daniells' landmark work, created more than a decade after *Views of Calcutta*. This later work has been described as 'the finest illustrated work ever published on India', in *The Reception of Blake in the Orient* published in 2006.

Not long after the completion of *Views of Calcutta*, Thomas began planning a voyage around India. The unpredictability of the Indian weather and the uncertainty of the river navigation made it a formidable venture. Regardless, the Daniells went ahead with their plan, earning the sobriquet 'artist-adventurers' in the process. As they travelled across the country, they drew whatever took their fancy, creating pencil sketches on the spot to be later completed into water colour. The scenes that they found more attractive or remarkable were chosen to be finished as oil paintings.

It is possible to accurately chart their progress from William's journal as well as the carefully notated drawings. Mildred Archer writes in her introduction to *Artist Adventurers in Eighteenth Century India: Thomas and William Daniell* published in 1974: 'Scarcely a day passed without sketches being made or worked up into full watercolours. Many of these are inscribed with titles and dates – those in ink being by Thomas and most of those in pencil by William. Together they form a vast pictorial record of the Daniells' itinerary.'

Their first tour was from Calcutta to Srinagar – in Pauri Garhwal district, not to be confused with the summer capital of Jammu and Kashmir – by boat. Though the preparation for the journey out of Calcutta had begun in late August, they were able to depart only by early September. They left Calcutta by boat on 3 September 1788, sailing upriver along the river Ganges.

Their route took the Daniells through breath-taking landscapes, including hills, dense jungles, populated villages and lands covered with ancient ruins. All the while, they were busy sketching the forts and palaces, the temples and tombs and of course the picturesque landscapes. In their selection of subjects to sketch, the duo was often guided by the paintings of Hodges.

They stopped for a day at Bhagalpur on 18 October 1788 to stay with a friend called Samuel Davis, who was an amateur artist. This break proved very helpful as Davis replenished their supplies for their onward journey, and also advised them on the route to take and places to visit on the way. They continued on to Kanpur and then travelled by road to Delhi. On the way they visited Agra, Fatehpur Sikri and Mathura, and reached Srinagar on 27th April 1789. The Daniells were the first Europeans to enter the city of Srinagar, and created a lot of interest amongst the locals. They also experienced some spectacular moments during this trip. We are told that while William was painting a picture of the Rope Bridge in Srinagar, Garhwal, they were informed that the city of Srinagar was being attacked by the Kumaon forces, and were asked to evacuate. However, William refused and continued painting. He commemorated the episode by naming the painting *'The Rope Bridge At Sirinagur, Over The Alucnindra, The Principal Branch Of The River Ganges'* and further added, 'Taken at the time of the evacuation of the/

City in consequence of the approach of/a large Army from Almorah. in the/Year 1789'.

At the end of an eventful stay at Srinagar, the Daniells began their return journey on 30th April 1789, stated by Archer in her 1980 book *Early Views of India*, taking a slightly different route and heading for Lucknow. They travelled for two months, stopping at a number of places before reaching Lucknow in July, by which time the monsoon had started. Spending the rainy season in Lucknow, they got acquainted with a French officer by the name of Claude Martin, who worked for the Nawab of Oudh, Asaf-ud-Daula. Martin welcomed the Daniells warmly and allowed them to stay with him. The duo used this time to finalize many of their paintings.

By the time the Daniells returned to Calcutta in November 1791, they had with them a substantial collection of oil paintings which they had decided to auction off. Soon after, they announced the auction in the *Calcutta Gazette*. The auction took place on 1 March 1792, and they succeeded in selling off their collection of 150 oil paintings.

With their finances replenished, the duo began preparing for a tour of south India – a rather daring plan as the southern part of the country was still unexplored territory when compared to eastern and northern India. Undeterred, the artist-adventurers set sail from Calcutta on 10 March 1792 and reached Madras a few days later on 29 March. The timing was fortunate for the Daniells, as their visit to south India coincided with the end of the third war between Tipu Sultan and the British. A major part of Sultan's territory had come under the control of the British, making their journey through this region much smoother and safer than it would otherwise have been. They stayed in Madras for 11 days before setting off on an exploration of the rest of the region on 9 April. From William's diaries, we know that during this journey they had access to a large retinue, including: two palanquins, each with bearers; two horses with grooms; a bullock cart; three pack-bullocks to carry tents and baggage; seven bearers to carry provisions; two porters to carry the drawing tables; and a staff of personal servants.

Their first stop was at Perambur, followed by another at Conjeevaram (Kanchipuram). At the latter spot they got their first glimpse of the magnificently carved temple there, which, according to William, was 'the most considerable we have seen', Archer mentions in *Early Views*. They were enthralled by the magnificent temples strewn across the entire region and tried to capture them on canvas along with the shrines and palaces all carved with thousands of intricate images.

Eventually, the Daniells reached Madura (Madurai) on 3 July. From there they travelled through the unchartered territories of the south, which abounded in spectacular natural scenery, till they reached the southernmost tip of India. They returned to Madras in November 1792.

Immediately, the duo made preparations to hold another auction, announcing it in the *Madras Courier* on 20 and 27 December. The auction was held on 18 February 1793 and was a success. They sold 68 oil paintings and eight drawings. They now had sufficient funds for their next, and final, tour.

By then, Thomas and William Daniell had been in India for seven years and had extensively covered the eastern, northern and southern parts of the country. All that remained was an exploration of western India. The duo set sail once more, this time heading for Bombay (now Mumbai).

Leaving Madras in mid-February 1793 on a country boat, they reached Bombay the following month. There, Thomas and William met an English artist by the name of James Wales, who acted as their tour guide and introduced them to the magnificent rock-cut temples of the region. They were particularly enthralled by Ellora, one of the largest rock-cut cave complexes in the world.

Unfortunately, Wales fell ill while at Kanheri Caves on Salsette Island. Despite being rushed back to Bombay, he died on 18 November 1795. Later, after their return to England, the Daniells engraved some of Wales's drawings and incorporated them in the sixth volume of *Oriental Scenery*.

The Daniells departed from India in May 1793, and arrived in England in September 1794. Once settled in London, they began preparations to publish a selection of their paintings of Indian scenes. They had brought back hundreds of artworks with them. Their collection included detailed drawings, watercolours accompanied by copious notes, and rough sketches made with the help of a camera obscura – which may be described as the ancestor of the photographic camera or, in other words, a nineteenth-century optical device often used by artists to make quick sketches in the field.

They began working on the engravings for their *Oriental Scenery* series of publications, turning a selection of their painting into aquatint prints. Even though William had mastered this new medium by then, it still required long hours of unremitting labour. According to another artist of the time by the name of Joseph Farington, William spent the first seven years after his return to England working from 6 a.m. until midnight.

The Daniells' magnum opus, *Oriental Scenery*, was released in 1795, initially as two volumes, each titled *Oriental Scenery: Twenty-four Views in Hindoostan*. Four more volumes were published by 1808. The series included a total of 144 coloured aquatints and 6 uncoloured titled-pages of the views of India. The complete set was priced at 220 guineas and sold well. The series was a huge success, both artistically and commercially, and was widely commended for its meticulous detail and realistic depictions.

Other projects undertaken by Thomas Daniell in England included *Picturesque Voyage to India, by Way of China* published in 1810. All his subsequent work continued to exhibit Eastern themes. Thomas associated himself with a number of landscape projects based on Indian subjects, the most well-known being his designing of the garden buildings of Sezincote for Sir Charles Cockerell, and an Indian temple for Sir John Osborne at Melchet Court.

Thomas and William also exhibited their paintings in prestigious galleries of England, including the Royal Academy and the British Institution. William set up his own line of business and went on voyages to Wales and Scotland. He began paintings on subjects other than India, with his most famous work of this period being *A Voyage Round Great Britain*. On 11 July 1801, William married Mary Westall, the eldest sister of artist Richard Westall, at Old Church St. Pancras, London. The couple had four daughters.

William Daniell died in Camden Town, London on 16 August 1837. He was 67 at the time. His uncle survived him by three years. In 1840, Thomas Daniell, still a bachelor, passed away in Kensington at the age of 91. Both uncle and nephew are buried in Kensal Green Cemetery in London.

One cannot help but admire and appreciate the amazing spirit, indomitable courage and tenacity of purpose the Daniells exhibited in travelling through unfamiliar, dangerous and uncharted terrain with limited resources, no knowledge of local languages and practically no support, financial or otherwise, from the government. They braved dense forests infested with wild animals and reptiles, crossed raging rivers and passed through battle-ravaged regions. To quote the *Oxford Dictionary of National Biography*, 'Thomas Daniell played an active role in graphically documenting a wide geographical and cultural range of sites across the Indian subcontinent, travelling more extensively than any of his contemporary colonial artists.'

Oriental Scenery has been widely acknowledged as the finest and most influential series of illustrations on India because these paintings succeeded in increasing the West's awareness and knowledge about India. However, equally important is the impact that the Daniells' paintings had on Indians themselves. Before the advent of the railways, the majority of Indians rarely ventured out of their own states. Thus, their idea about India was limited to what they might have read in books or travel writings. Therefore, someone belonging to the north would not have any idea about the exquisiteness of the temple architecture of the south, or someone from the east would have no visual reference of the beauty of the Taj Mahal. This was changed after the publication of *Oriental Scenery*.

It is interesting to note that the influence of *Oriental Scenery* was felt in some unexpected areas as well. Following the publication of these prints, oriental motifs began to appear in British homes, and were seen on wallpapers, on ceramics and potteries, and other assorted curios. It set off a fashion trend in nineteenth-century England for Indian-inspired designs. Some of the areas in which the influence of *Oriental Scenery* was most pronounced were architecture, landscape gardens and interior decorations. Many new buildings constructed at the time featured architectural styles from the Daniells' aquatints, including domes, arches and large heavy pillars harking back the rock-cut temples of western India.

Probably one of the most outstanding examples of this synthesis is the Warren Hastings memorial monument erected in 1800 at the university chapel at Oxford, in Melchet Park. Built in the form of a beautiful 'Hindoo' temple, it depicts the bust of Warren Hastings rising out of the sacred lotus flower. The monument was based on a painting by Thomas Daniell (Plate 11 of the first set of *Oriental Scenery*). The original aquatint had been inspired by a temple that the Daniells had chanced upon inside the majestic hill fort of Rohtasgarh during their tour of northern India.

Another great example of Indian-inspired architecture is the unique Sezincote House in Gloucestershire, England. The building and landscape gardens of Sezincote were designed by Charles Cockerell in 1805 in the style of the Indian palaces of the sixteenth and seventeenth centuries, complete with copper domes and minarets. The building is surrounded by an Eastern-influenced garden that featured a Hindu temple dedicated to Surya, the sun god.

Father Dr John Felix Raj, SJ, a Jesuit priest, as well as the Founder, Vice-Chancellor and a professor of economics at St. Xavier's University, Kolkata and former Vice-Principal, Rector and Principal of St. Xavier's College, Kolkata, has this to say:

> More than any other work of art produced at the turn of the 19th century, *Oriental Scenery* contributed the most to the dispersal of knowledge about Indian history, architecture and geography, while at the same time demonstrating that Indian subjects could be artistically reconciled with an essentially European aesthetic. The Daniells must be credited with truly popularizing the Indian style and their aquatints served as a fertile source for a whole host of imitations in England and on the continent.

6

HENRY THOMAS COLEBROOKE

The Founder of True Sanskrit Scholarship in Europe

'His (Colebrooke's) literary and scientific labours were immense. A great mathematician, a zealous astronomer and profound Sanskrit scholar, his writings always commanded the highest attention: he has been described as facile princeps among Sanskrit scholars. He wrote also on the Vedas, on Sanskrit grammar, and a lexicon, on the Sect of Jains, on Indian Jurisprudence and Roman law, besides other papers on Hindu law, philosophy and customs, Indian Algebra, on Astronomy, the height of the Himalayas, Botany, Geology, Comparative Philology, etc...'

– Charles Edward Buckland[1]

Winter of 1783

SIR GEORGE COLEBROOKE, ERSTWHILE CHAIRMAN OF THE EAST India Company, was at his home reading a letter from his son

[1] As found in the *Dictionary of Indian Biography* by Charles Edward Buckland published in 1968.

Henry Thomas. The letter was sent from Calcutta. 'It would alarm you,' Henry wrote, '(if you could) transport yourself for an instant to this place...' This place, of course, referred to India. The tone of the letter was dark and melancholic. This letter, and many others, were collected and published in the article 'Notices of the Life of Henry Thomas Colebrooke, Esq., by His Son' in 1839.

The reason for Henry's discontent was that he was still unemployed despite 10 months of being in India. It was unheard of for an Englishman not to find employment in India, and it was even more incredible when the man in question happened to be the son of the ex-chairman of the East India Company! Henry's father, George Colebrooke, 2nd Baronet of Gatton in Surrey, came from an old and wealthy firm of bankers. He was chairman of the East India Company and a Member of the British Parliament. He inherited £2,00,000 from his father-in-law, but went bankrupt because of imprudent investments. He had retired to Boulogne after the East India Company granted him a pension of £200 per annum.

However, Sir George's enormous influence within the Court of Directors, and his very cordial terms with Warren Hastings, governor-general of India, had not been able to procure even a mid-level position with the Company for Henry. Sir George blamed himself for the fiasco. He should have known better than send his son to India at a time when there was a widespread disillusionment with the functioning of the East India Company following the passing of the Regulating Act in the British Parliament in June 1773. The Act had been passed by the British Parliament following the corruption and misgovernment by the East India Company, particularly in Bengal. It was the first parliamentary ratification and authorization defining the powers and authority of the East India Company in context of its Indian possessions. Sir George should have anticipated the consequence of the Act, which had drastically limited the authority and the powers of the Company. As a consequence, the governor-general's position had become extremely shaky. Besides, Hastings himself was in the midst of a raging controversy at that time.

The apprehension that the Company would now be deprived of political patronage had begun to spread amongst a majority of the members of the civil service, causing widespread disgruntlement. Sir George had failed to read the writing on the wall, and it was only through his son's letter that he understood the situation in India. Henry had written about the times where jobs had been promised but nothing had materialized because the Board had just sat on them, without passing any decision. In his published letters, he also mentioned the time when a certain employee had tried to take up the matter with the Board of Directors of the East India Company, he was told sternly that 'his spirited conduct might cost him the service'.

When Henry was a young boy, he had been scholarly, but a recluse. Young Henry had seldom participated in any of the usual amusements of childhood. In fact, he was rather precocious and used to tell his siblings that his habits and taste were that of a cleric, and that he was best suited for the profession of a clergyman. Sir George's hope that things would change after his son's arrival in India had not fructified. In fact, his disappointment had only deepened by a derisive comment made by Henry, assuring him that there was no danger of his ever applying too intensely to the study of Indian languages.

Sir George thought his dream of seeing his son becoming an oriental scholar and following in the footsteps of Jones would not become reality. Indeed, during his early years in India, Henry was disdainful of oriental scholars and referred to them as 'nothing less than pedantic pretenders' in his letters. If someone had told Sir George then that his son would one day be acknowledged as a master of Sanskrit, he would likely not have believed it.

Yet, Henry Thomas Colebrooke was destined to become, in the words of Max Müller, quoted by O.P. Kejariwal in *The Asiatic Society of Bengal and the Discovery of India's Past, 1784-1838* published in 1988, 'the greatest oriental scholar that England has ever produced'. The story of his transformation from a reluctant orientalist to 'the first great Sanskrit scholar in Europe' is a fascinating one.

Born in London on 15 June 1765, Henry Thomas Colebrooke was the third son of Sir George Colebrooke and Mary Gaynor of Antigua. From the age of 12 to 16, Henry lived in France with his family. He was never sent to a regular school; instead, he studied at home with a tutor. Later in life, he would often cite this fact as a testimony of the advantages of home-schooling. Henry, on his own, studied a wide variety of subjects and, as per Prof. S. Ramaswami Iyengar in *Eminent Orientalists* published in 2000, by the time he was 17, 'he possessed as much knowledge was as might be expected of a graduate of a university.' He was proficient in mathematics, had a good knowledge of Greek and Roman classics and had mastered the French and German languages.

In August 1782, at 17, he secured a writership in the Bengal service due to his father's influence. He arrived in India in April 1783, and was received by his brother Sir Edward Colebrooke in Calcutta. Edward was already living in India, and initially Henry lived with his brother's family in Calcutta.

As his early letters to his father show, Henry found no employment for nearly 10 months. Those letters reflect the general mood of discontent among the Company employees during that time. 'India is no longer the mine of gold,' he wrote, 'Everyone is disgusted and all whose affairs permit abandon it as fast as possible.' It was evident from his letters that Henry himself had started thinking of returning home. He even hinted that he could become a farmer and settle in rural England.

After almost a year's wait, when Henry finally found employment, it was in a lowly position in the board of accounts. After working for three years in Calcutta, he was transferred to Tirhoot in Bihar in 1786. He remained in this department for nearly nine years, working as assistant collector of revenue. His move to Tirhoot brought about a change in his life, but not the change that his father had been hoping for. Instead of turning to research and studies, Henry began spending his time playing sports. Every time his father tried to get him interested in the literature and religion of the East, Henry cut him short with the excuse that his new pastime coupled with his official duties left him little time for literary pursuits.

What was even more disconcerting for Sir George was that his son continued to be scornful towards everything oriental.

Henry was particularly disdainful of translations, which he felt was meant for only those who needed to fill their purses. He referred to Wilkins as 'Sanskrit-mad', the Asiatic Miscellany as 'a repository of nonsense', and the Institute of Akbar as 'a dunghill, in which perhaps a pearl or two might be found.'

The first sign of change in Henry's attitude can be seen in the late 1780s when, in one of the letters to his father, he admitted that though he was still not keen on translations, he was not averse to working on some subject relevant to India, specifically on 'original compositions on Oriental history and sciences'. However, he was reticent about taking up such a project because he felt that it 'required more reading in the literature of the East' than he possessed or was likely to attain.

Things took another turn in April 1789 when he was posted as assistant collector in Purnea, Bihar. The collector under whom he had to work there was extremely indolent and apathetic, and was happy to hand over the everyday duties of the station to his assistant. Henry did not mind this, and began work at his new post with great zest.

His first task in Purnea was to make a first-hand study of the agriculture of Bengal, an area yet to be studied. Henry worked enthusiastically on this project and soon his hard work, perseverance and efficiency was noticed by the colonial government. Not long afterwards, he was assigned to investigate the resources of that collectorate and prepare a report on how the government could boost its revenue in Bengal.

This job brought Henry into direct contact with the local peasants for the first time, and he became extremely interested in the study of the agriculture, trade and industry of Bengal. Though official duties took up a big chunk of his time, he began spending all his spare hours in collecting huge amounts of data related to his subject. Ultimately, he had enough information to bring out his very first publication: *Remarks on the Present State of the Husbandry and Commerce of Bengal.* Privately published in 1795, the book was an in-depth investigation of the pathetic condition of the state of agriculture and commerce in India. It contained some scathing criticism of the commercial policies of the East India Company while advocating the abolition of the Company's monopoly. It was one of the first occasions when free trade with India was seriously proposed.

Unsurprisingly, a mid-level Company employee daring to censure its policy stirred up a hornet's nest. Considering the dictatorial authority exercised by the Company over its employees, it was indeed a foolhardy act on the part of Henry Colebrooke. Soon after its publication, Henry tried to find out how the book had been received. He writes in a letter that he was ticked off by a Company officer, who told him curtly, 'You may think yourself fortunate if you remain in the service.' However, thanks to his father's influence, Henry remained unscathed.

It was only after a decade of living in India that Henry Colebrooke finally found the desire to know more about the country. He developed an interest about ancient India, and started learning Sanskrit, Arabic and Persian. He was particularly fascinated by Sanskrit and was determined to acquire a deeper knowledge of the language than his contemporaries had. This led him to embark on a serious course of study which was to occupy him completely until his return to Europe.

Henry had become aware of the importance of Sanskrit for acquiring a proper knowledge of Indian law, so he had no choice but to learn the language in order to fulfil his legal functions. This need for understanding the Hindu lawbooks was what gave him the initial push to begin his Sanskrit studies. He began with an extensive study of the ancient Smriti literature, a branch of the Vedas relating to law and social conduct.

Though Henry had begun the study of Sanskrit while in Purnea, it was only after he was transferred to Natore (present-day Bangladesh) that he took it up with passion. However, his initial attempts to learn the language had been frustrating. He had to abandon his studies twice before he finally succeeded. It is interesting to note that his experience of learning Sanskrit was very different from some of his contemporaries. He was pleasantly surprised to find that the pandits were willing to support him wholeheartedly in his endeavour, and did not display the antagonism faced by some of the other orientalists.

In one of the letters to his father, Henry mentioned that he could not understand why it was assumed that the brahmins were averse to instruct strangers, since in his experience many Englishmen who had studied the language found 'the greatest readiness in them to give us access to all their sciences. They (the pandits) do not even conceal from us the most sacred text of their Vedas.'

Henry Colebrooke's study of Sanskrit eventually became far more extensive than any other orientalist of the period.

He did not confine himself to any particular subject, instead attempting to 'skim the surface of all their sciences'. The remarkable shift in his perception in relation to Sanskrit studies can be gauged from the letter he wrote to his father in December 1793: 'The further our literary inquiries are extended here, the more vast and stupendous is the scene which opens to us...' One can only imagine the satisfaction his father would have had from this transformation in his son.

One of the subjects of Henry's research during this time was the Hindu social issue of sati or 'suttee', the practice of widow self-immolation. It resulted in a short paper titled 'Ceremonies observed by Hindu women burning themselves with the corpse of their deceased husbands'. The report was based on various Sanskrit texts, and was published in 1794 in *Asiatic Researches.* This was Henry's very first contribution to the journal and received enthusiastic commendation from Jones.

Following the death of Sir William Jones, Henry Colebrooke's life took another turn in the summer of 1794. The direction of his studies changed from random reading to focused research, as can be seen from a letter to his father in which he writes, 'I am now fairly entered among oriental researches... and Sanscrit inquiries'.

It might be recalled that in 1776, Nathaniel Brassey Halhed had published the translation *A Code of Gentoo Laws, or, Ordinations of the Pandits,* which had not been a direct translation from the original Sanskrit (Vivādārṇavasetu). It had been translated from Sanskrit into Persian by brahmin scholars, and then from Persian into English by Nathaniel Brassey

Halhed. Many felt that this double process of interpretation was likely to have taken away from the reliability of the book. Therefore, Jones, under the aegis of the government, had agreed to have a more extensive and authentic compilation made.

The task of compiling the Hindu Laws in Sanskrit was now entrusted to Jagannath Tarka Panchanan of Tribeni in Bengal, a renowned pandit and a friend of Jones, who was to take on the task of translating this work into English. However, the project did not go much beyond the planning stage because of Jones's premature death in April 1794. The laborious task of translating the 'copious digest of Hindu law' from Sanskrit to English then fell on Henry Colebrooke, as mentioned by him in a letter dated October 1794.

The magnitude and the importance of the project can be understood from the terms and conditions offered to Henry for the task. The stipulations required him to give up his current position and take up residence in Calcutta till the work was completed. He was to be given a salary for the period. Though keen to take up this project, Henry was not too enthusiastic about these terms.

Instead, he offered to carry out the work to its completion at his own leisure. This alternative was accepted, and Henry wrote about it to his father, saying that though the work would be voluminous, he expected 'to finish it in six months'. However, he had miscalculated the extent of labour required for the project, and it took him more than two years to complete the work.

For compiling *Vivada-Bhangarnava*, a digest of Hindu Law in Sanskrit, Panchanan was paid a salary of Rs 300 per month, a princely sum in that era. His team of assistants were each paid Rs 100 monthly. Once the Sanskrit was compiled, Henry Colebrooke began to work on the difficult task of translating it into English. His gruelling work schedule made his friends apprehensive for his health.

While still working on the translation, Henry was appointed as the magistrate of Mirzapur, near Benares, the great centre of Brahmanical learning. This gave further impetus to his Sanskrit studies. His reaction to this posting is recorded in the letter he sent to his father from Rajshahi on 11 August 1795: 'It will afford you pleasure to learn that I have been appointed to an eligible post, the Adawlut at Mirzapoor. From its neighbourhood to Benares, I shall have the convenience for which I wish to be placed at that city, — ready access to the Hindu College... My pursuits in Sanscrit, in which I am confident you equally interest yourself for my success, proceed well.'

On 3 January 1797, Henry completed the translation. With a tremendous sense of relief, he announced to his father: 'The task of translating the digest of Indian law, on which I have been so long employed, is now completed. Last week I sent it to the Governor General.' The work was published as *A Digest of Hindu Law on Contracts and Successions,* with a commentary by Panchanan. *Digest of Hindu Law* received high praise from the governor-general, and James Prinsep eulogized it as 'a standing monument of the professional value of the writer, and of his skill at the same time as a jurist and an oriental scholar', as published in *The Asiatic Journal and Monthly Register for British and Foreign India, China, and Australia* from 1838.

Another significant development during this period was the casting of types in Calcutta for printing the Sanskrit language. This gave an additional boost to the study of Sanskrit. Colebrooke began planning a Sanskrit grammar to accompany the dictionary of Sanskrit that a friend of his was preparing for the press. He hoped that with these texts that Sanskrit might be taken up for study in the universities of England.

Around 1798, Henry's interest turned towards the study of literature and science. It began after he was sent to Nagpur, where he was stationed for two years. Nagpur, in present day Maharashtra state, was taken over by the British East India Company in the nineteenth century and made the capital of the Central Provinces and Berar. In 1801, he was appointed judge of the Sadr Diwani Adalat, the supreme court of revenue in British India established at Calcutta by Warren Hastings in 1772. In appreciation of his work on the *Digest* as well as his competence as a judge, he was nominated to a seat on the bench of the new court of appeal at Calcutta. He became the president of the bench in 1805. Towards the end of that year, he was promoted to the post of chief judge of Sadr Diwani Adalat. This gave Henry more leisure hours than he had in his previous roles, and allowed him to devote more time to the study of oriental literature and sciences. According to M. Monocalm's 1995 book *The Origin of Thought and Speech*, the French historian and philosopher Voltaire had declared that the Veda was 'the most precious gift for which the West had ever been indebted to the East.' Though Henry had plans of presenting three or four essays to the Asiatic Society in 1801, he was still unsure about himself, and reticent about writing on the Vedas. However, he continued an exhaustive study of the subject, and through dogged determination and untiring effort, accomplished the seemingly impossible task of wading through the vast and complex Sanskrit commentaries in the Vedas. He eventually presented his landmark paper *Essay on the Veda,* which was hailed as the 'most important desideratum in Indian literature', as quoted by Rosane and Ludo Rocher in their book *The Making of Western Indology* published in 2014. According to British orientalist Horace Hayman Wilson, as mentioned in the article 'Notices', Henry Colebrooke's essay on the Vedas is 'still the only authority available for information respecting the oldest and most important religious writings of the Hindus.' This essay was the first authentic account of these ancient scriptures, and laid the foundation of the Western world's interest in these ancient texts.

Henry was made a member of the supreme council of the governor-general from 1807 to 1812, while retaining his seat in the Sadr court. At the end of five years, he became a member of the board of revenue. Lord Wellesley honoured Henry by appointing him as an honorary professor of Hindu law and Sanskrit at Fort William College (the institution established in Calcutta by Lord Wellesley in 1800 for the education of civil servants). In this unpaid post, Henry acted as an academic director and as an examiner.

Though he took no active part in teaching, Henry's connection with the college led to the compilation of his Sanskrit grammar. The first volume of this work was completed and published in 1805. However, the publication of two other Sanskrit grammars during this period – one by

Dr Carey and the other by Sir Charles Wilkins – resulted in Henry abandoning his project.

In 1810, Henry Colebrook published translations from Sanskrit to English of two celebrated treatises on the Hindu Law of inheritance, *Mitākṣarā* and *Dāyabhāga. Mitākṣarā* was the translation of a legal commentary on 'inheritance by birth' by prominent twelfth-century jurist Vijnaneshwara; and *Dāyabhāga* was a treatise on Hindu laws of inheritance written by Jīmūtavāhana, a twelfth-century writer of legal and religious treatises.

The main difference between the two texts is based on when children get to inherit their parents' property. According to *Dāyabhāga*, the children get the right to the property only after the death of the parents, whereas *Mitākṣarā* gives the children the right to ancestral property right from birth. These treatises continued to be used in the law courts of India and acted as the principal guide for laws on inheritance until the enactment of the Hindu Succession Act in 1956.

While Henry valued this translation work as much as, if not more than, any of his other legal writings, the publication did not get the response he had expected. He was sorely disappointed that it was more or less ignored by the public and was never in much demand.

Through his numerous essays, Colebrooke succeeded in presenting aspects of the Indian culture hitherto unknown to the Western world. His writings covered diverse subjects. His essays included 'State of Science as known to the Hindus', *Essays on the Religious Ceremonies of the Hindus,* 'On the Indian and Arabic Divisions of the Zodiac', 'On the Notions of Hindu Astronomers concerning the Procession of the Equinoxes and Motions of the Planets', 'On the Origin of Caste', *The Amara Cosha, a Sanskrit Lexicon*, 'Algebra, with Arithmetic and Mensuration', and more.

His essay titled 'The Sanskrit and Prakrit Languages', written in 1810 for the Asiatic Society, was an attempt to analyse the Hindu vernaculars. He came to the remarkable conclusions that Hindi was a separate language and not a derivative of Persianized Urdu, and that Hindi as a language existed even before Urdu. The publication of this paper is a clear indication that he was bringing within the ambit of his study a wide range of Hindi literature.

Henry Colebrooke was one of the first Western scholars to point to the existence of a Jain tradition. In his essay 'Observations on the Sect of the Jains', he wrote in details about the beliefs and practices of the Jain community, which at that time was not really known outside India. He also conducted one of the earliest studies on the Bohra community and wrote a paper titled 'The Origin and Peculiar Tenets of Certain Mohammedan Sects'. According to this paper, the Bohras were natives of Gujarat who had converted to Islam a few centuries earlier.

Before Colebrooke, the inscription on the Delhi iron pillar had been copied by Colonel Polier, a Swiss adventurer, art collector, and military engineer who was in India around 1716, and translated by Jones with the help of a pandit; however, due to inaccurate copying, the inscription was wrongly dated as 67 CE. However, another copy was made by Captain James Hoare and that revealed the error: it had been inscribed in 1164 CE. Colebrooke translated the inscription that extolled the Vigrah Raja, king of Sakambari; this was the same Hindu king who was later identified as the famous king, Prithviraj Chauhan.

Another lesser-known aspect of Henry's temperament was his immense fascination with the Himalayas; he fondly referred to them as 'my mountains'. He was especially interested in calculating the heights of the mountains. During his days in Purnea in the early 1790s, he began a series of observations to establish the height of the range. After deducing an average height of 26,000 feet, Henry brought this matter to the notice of his cousin, Robert Colebrooke. Robert was an ex-soldier serving as the surveyor-general of Bengal in 1794.

The only way to access the highest peaks was through the Kingdom of Nepal. However, at the time, the Nepal border was closed. Robert travelled to reach Pilibhit, where he took a series of observations of the snow-capped peaks. Unfortunately, during the course of this expedition, Robert died of malarial fever on 21 September 1807. At that time Henry was in Bhagalpur, where, in 1784, Sir William Jones had beheld the Himalayas and had declared, that there was 'abundant reason to think that we saw from Bhagilpoor, the highest mountains in the world', according to Lord Teignmouth's *Memoirs of the Life, Writings and Correspondence, of Sir William Jones* published in 1806.

It might have been a guess for Jones but for Henry Colebrooke it was a matter of conviction. He felt that he owed it to his cousin's memory to present an overwhelming case for the Himalayas to be recognized as the tallest mountain range in the world. To this end, he collected the testimony of all the earlier travellers into Tibet and laboured for the next seven years on his outstanding thesis 'On the Height of the Himalaya Mountains', published in twelfth volume of the *Asiatic Researches* in 1818. Henry concluded his paper with the following observation: 'I consider the evidence to be now sufficient to authorize an unreserved declaration of the opinion, that the Himalayas is the loftiest range of Alpine mountains which has yet been noticed, its most elevated peaks greatly exceeding the highest of the Andes.' Henry Colebrooke was the first European to recognize the Himalayas as the loftiest mountain range in the world.

In 1810, Henry married Elizabeth Wilkinson. The couple had three sons, but Elizabeth passed away in 1814. Henry then left India with his sons, and arrived back England in 1815. He had spent 32 years in India.

Initially residing with his mother near Bath, Henry then moved back to London, where he spent the rest of his life on scholarly researches. He worked using the treasured collection of original manuscripts and copies that he had brought from India. In 1818, he presented 2,749 documents from his valuable collection of Sanskrit manuscripts to the East India Company's library (now India Office Library) in London. Max Müller describes these documents, in his *Chips from a German Workshop* published in 1876, as a 'treasury from which every student of Sanskrit has since drawn'.

Henry Colebrooke became a member of almost every scientific institution in London and passed a considerable portion of his hours with these societies. At this period, he wrote largely on scientific subjects and was a frequent contributor to the 'Quarterly Journal of Science'. He was one of the founders of the Astronomical Society of London, which became the Royal Astronomical Society after receiving the Royal Charter in 1831.

For several years, Henry toyed with the idea of establishing an association modelled on the Asiatic Society of Calcutta. Finally, in 1823, he invited a number of likeminded people to his home and mooted the idea. Since all those who were present had retired from the East India Company and had also been associated with the Asiatic Society of Calcutta, the idea of establishing such a society in London was warmly welcomed.

After a number of preliminary meetings, on 15 March 1823 the foundation of the Asiatic Society of Great Britain and Ireland was laid at the Thatched House Tatvern on St. James' Street, London. In 1824, King George IV granted the Royal Charter to the society, and from August 1824, it became known as the Royal Asiatic Society (RAS).

At the inaugural meeting of the society which was recorded in the first volume of the *Transactions of the Royal Asiatic Society of Great Britain and Ireland*, Colebrooke delivered a speech outlining the association's aims, in which he said, 'Nothing which has much engaged the thoughts of man is foreign to our enquiry... We do not exclude from our research the political transactions of Asiatic states, nor the lucubrations of Asiatic philosophers.'

The speech was on the same lines as Jones's inaugural exposition in the Asiatic Society. This was followed up with the publication of the first volume of the 'Transactions of the Royal Asiatic Society', which later became the 'Journal of the

Royal Asiatic Society'. These journals too were very much on the lines of *Asiatic Researches.* The members included a long list of luminaries, including Sir Charles Wilkins.

While Henry declined to be the president, he remained active as a director of the society, contributing numerous articles to its transactions, doing his best to promote Sanskrit in England. It was his hope that Sanskrit would be taken up for study in the universities of England. He wrote extensively during this period but his most important work was no doubt *The Philosophy of the Hindus in its Five Principal Divisions*. Prinsep was convinced that these five essays were immeasurably superior to anything published before on the same subject.

Henry continued to zealously promote the study of ancient Indian literature and sciences till 1830, when his infirmity compelled him to resign from his duties at the Royal Asiatic Society. The last years of Henry's life were beset with misfortune. He suffered heavy financial losses and became involved in family litigations. Then the deaths of his two adult sons and two nieces took their toll on his health and broke his spirits. Towards the end, he developed cataract, for which there was no treatment those days. He became almost totally blind. He passed away on 10 March 1837, at the age of 72.

Henry Colebrooke brought to the notice of the Western world the most ancient works, particularly the various sciences, of the Hindus. Apart from his famous dissertation on the Vedas, he also comprehensively studied ancient Hindu algebra, geometry and arithmetic – the first European to do so. From the original Sanskrit, he translated papers such as 'State of Science as known to the Hindus' and 'Algebra, with Arithmetic and Mensuration'. These brought to light the fact that mathematical science was in a state of high development in India long before the Europeans learned the mere rudiments from the Arabs or the Greeks. His three-part *Essays on the Religion and Philosophy of the Hindus,* along with his articles on Sanskrit and Prakrit, were 'sufficient to place the author, in the highest rank of oriental scholars – and which must long continue to form the best textbooks of those who wish to investigate the depths of Indian literature and religion', according to the sixth volume of the 'Journal of the Asiatic Society of Bengal' published in 1837.

To really appreciate Henry's legacy we need to keep in mind that he was writing at a time when Indian scholarship was being viewed with suspicion; the reason for this was that many Europeans who could not study from the original manuscripts had been misled by pandits, who often fed them with what they thought that the foreigners wanted to hear. As a result, the writings were flawed and many intellectuals began to doubt the very existence of the Vedas. And some, like Scottish philosopher and mathematician Dugald Stewart, even went to the extent of saying that Sanskrit was probably a fiction made up by the brahmins!

J.D. Pearson, the celebrated librarian of the School of Oriental and African Studies at London University, said in volume 25 of 'The Asiatic Journal for British India and its Dependencies': 'Colebrooke's profound knowledge of all Indian subjects, literature and science, combined with the union of the most extensive erudition with the most chastened judgment and an accurate scientific acquaintance with several subjects... are unsurpassed by those of any other contributor to our researches.' It was Henry's scientific temperament and moderate writing tone that convinced people of the accuracy of his statements. He influenced an entire generation of Europeans and laid the foundation of the Western world's interest in these ancient texts.

According to Prinsep, mentioned in the sixth volume of the society's journal, the reason for Colebrooke's popularity was that while reading his dissertation 'the reader feels that it is not a mere philologist or collector of ancient records that he is consulting but one whose critical sagacity weighs well with the value of the age, and the import of every authority that he alleges: and whose statements in consequence, may be received with the most entire respect and confidence.'

According to this son T.E. Colebrooke's *The Life of H.T. Colebrooke* published in 1873, Colebrooke regarded himself as having picked up the torch of scholarly interest in India's culture, religions and languages from Jones and as passing this on to Wilson, to whom he wrote in 1827:

> Careless and indifferent as our countrymen are, I think, nevertheless, you and I may derive more complacent feelings from the reflection that, following the footsteps of Sir W. Jones, we have, with so little aid of collaborators, and so little encouragement, opened nearly every avenue, and left it to foreigners, who are taking up the clue we have furnished, to complete the outline of what we have sketched. It is some gratification to natural pride that the opportunity which the English have enjoyed has not been wholly unemployed.

In the 1870s, Buckland notes in *Dictionary* that Müller eulogized Colebrooke's genius, referring to him as 'the *facile princeps* among Sanskrit scholars' and 'father and founder of true Sanskrit scholarship in Europe, and upholder of the antiquity of Indian scientific knowledge'.

7

HORACE HAYMAN WILSON

In Defence of Hinduism

'Of all the Orientalists during the early history of the movement, Horace H. Wilson was undoubtedly its most prolific scholar and most articulate spokesman; he was also a leading social activist on behalf of Hindu modernism in Bengal. One should add that he was unique among Orientalists, in his critical defence of Hinduism in all its aspects: classical, medieval and modern.'

– David Kopf[1]

March 1832, Calcutta

THE SELECTION OF THE BODEN PROFESSOR OF SANSKRIT HAD generated much interest amongst scholars and intellectuals, and there had been a lot of excitement surrounding the selection. It had been a close contest between the three candidates who were all established names in the field of Oriental languages:

---

[1] From 'The Historiography of British Orientalism, 1772–1992' in *Objects of Enquiry: The Life, Contributions, and Influence of Sir William Jones (1746-1794)* edited by Garland Cannon and Kevin R. Brine, published in 1995.

Horace Hayman Wilson, who was a renowned Sanskrit scholar; Sir Graves Chamney Haughton, a scholar of Oriental languages and professor of Hindu literature at the East India Company College in Hailebury; and William Hodge Mill, a churchman and an erudite orientalist who was the first principal of Bishop's College in Calcutta. The final selection was to be done by the main governing body of the university, comprising all who had graduated with a master's degree or a doctorate.

Although Wilson had placed an advertisement outlining his suitability for the post in the *Times*, he had not been too confident about the outcome of the election. He knew that he was distrusted by some in the university for being too close to Hindu leaders. His avant-garde lifestyle was viewed with suspicion, and his links to the theatrical world in Calcutta were considered to be disreputable. Another factor that was likely to go against him was his long-term liaison with an Indian woman, with whom he was believed to have had two sons.

However, he got unexpected relief when Haughton, who had been a former pupil of Wilson, volunteered to withdraw from the election. Another factor that impacted the voting was Wilson's letter addressed to the members of convocation resident in Trinity College, Oxford, announcing himself as a candidate. The letter stated that Wilson had begun studying Sanskrit, having been inspired by Sir William Jones, and that in 1813, he had published a translation of a short poem by Kalidasa titled *Meghadoota or Cloud Messenger* with the aim of creating interest in the study of Sanskrit. The letter also mentioned that the translation had been appreciated by no less a person than the famous Sanskrit scholar Henry Colebrooke.

Colebrook and Wilson were together in India for about six years, from 1808 to 1814. It is likely that Colebrooke's support clinched the election in Wilson's favour – according to the *Times*, he won by a narrow margin, securing 207 votes to Mill's 200. Thus, in 1832, Oxford University selected Horace Hayman Wilson to be the first Boden Professor of Sanskrit. This was a richly deserved honour. Besides being an outstanding Sanskrit scholar, Wilson was a linguist, historian, chemist, accountant, numismatist, actor and musician all rolled into one.

However, one of the most interesting aspects of his life is that, unlike his illustrious predecessors, Horace Hayman Wilson had no background in classical literature. In fact, he began his career as a medical doctor. How did a young Englishman trained to become a medical doctor end up becoming one of the most distinguished orientalists of England?

Horace Hayman Wilson was born on 26 September 1786 in London to George Paterson and Miss Woolston. Right from his childhood, Horace displayed an inquisitive mind and an insatiable urge for gaining knowledge in different subjects. Even as a young boy in school, he used his vacation time to learn about chemical analysis and the property of metals from his uncle, who worked in the assay department of the government mint. Horace became fascinated with assaying, which is the process by which a metal is chemically tested to determine its qualities. This training was to stand him in good stead in his career.

Wilson studied medicine at St. Thomas's Hospital and qualified as a surgeon. After qualifying as a medical doctor, he was appointed assistant surgeon with the East India Company and left England for Calcutta in 1808. Due to some mishaps, the voyage took about six months, which was longer than usual. This caused a great deal of consternation amongst the passengers, but Wilson utilized this time to learn Hindustani from a learned Hindu gentleman who was travelling in the same ship. He finally reached Calcutta in March 1809. He was 23.

However, soon after his arrival in Calcutta, Wilson was informed that Dr John Leyden, under whom he was supposed to serve as a surgeon, had been appointed the assay master for the Calcutta Mint. Wilson would still serve as his assistant, but as the deputy assay master. It is strange that two doctors of Medicine in the service of the East India Company should be put to work in a mint. This incident is a revelation on the unquestioning loyalty displayed by the employees of the Company.

Things took another unexpected turn when the war with the Dutch broke out in 1811. Dr Leyden was deputed to accompany the expedition to Java, Indonesia, as an interpreter between the Dutch and the British. However, he fell ill there, and died. As a result, Wilson was appointed to the post of assay master of the Calcutta Mint. He held this position for the rest of his stay in India.

Wilson was also appointed as secretary to the mint committee. During this period, he used all his spare time to brush up his knowledge of numismatics, another subject that he was passionate about. The in-depth knowledge of the subject acquired by him during this period helped him many years later to write *Ariana Antiqua*, his famous book on the coins of Afghanistan.

While in India, Wilson became acquainted with Charles Wilkins and Henry Colebrooke, who were already in the country doing pioneering work in Oriental studies. Deeply inspired by the works of these Sanskrit scholars, he turned his attention to the study of Sanskrit and other ancient languages, and literature of India. His tremendous enthusiasm attracted the attention of Colebrooke, who recommended Wilson's name for appointment to the post of secretary of the Asiatic Society of Bengal in 1811.

Wilson held the post for 21 years, during which time he assiduously promoted Indian scholarship, acquisition of Indian texts for the Asiatic Society library, and interactions between English orientalists and Indian intellectuals in Calcutta. He published a number of scholarly papers in *Asiatic Researches*.

Within four years of his arrival in Calcutta, Wilson's very first literary effort took shape. It was the translation of Kalidasa's *Meghadoota or Cloud Messenger*, and was highly acclaimed by scholars. Colebrooke complimented him, as quoted in volume seven of *The Asiatic Journal and Monthly Register for British and Foreign India, China, and Australia*, saying, 'I am surprised at the great closeness to the original which you have been able to preserve in an elegant poetical translation. It conveys a much nearer idea of the original than any prose version can do.'

Wilson then began to work on a monumental project: the first Sanskrit-English dictionary. It was a mammoth task for which he worked along with local scholars while also doing his own research. The dictionary was published in 1819, and placed Wilson in the first rank of Sanskrit scholars.

Soon after Wilson completed the first Sanskrit-English dictionary towards the end of 1819, he was sent by the government to Benares for the inspection of the Sanskrit College. This college had been was established in 1791–92 by Jonathan Duncan, the East India Company Resident in Benares to promote the study of Hindu laws and philosophy in the city.

Wilson streamlined the administration of the institution during his one-year stay at Benares, and also used the time there to further his knowledge of Sanskrit with the help of some of the most-learned pandits of the city. He focused his studies on the dramatic literature of the Hindus.

Wilson enjoyed plays and the theatre world, and established Chowringhee Theatre in Calcutta as a venue to showcase his histrionic talents and musical skills. It was the best-known English theatre set up by the efforts of Wilson along with the renowned Sanskrit scholar D.L. Richardson and Dwarkanath Tagore, the grandfather of Rabindranath Tagore. Wilson also studied and collected material for his writings on Sanskrit plays. It took him a few years to complete translations in prose and verse of six Sanskrit plays, which he published as *Hindu Theatre* in 1826. The book included analytical descriptions and specimens of 23 other dramatic compositions. It received rave reviews in Europe and was translated into French and German.

In 1828, shortly after the release of *Hindu Theatre*, Wilson published *A Descriptive Catalogue of the Oriental Manuscripts and Other Articles of the late Colonel Colin Mackenzie* – who was a Scottish army officer in the East India Company, and a collector of antiques – with an introductory view of language, literature, religion and history of the Indian peninsula. A year later, on 11 March 1829, Wilson tied the knot with Frances Sarah Parr Siddons, who was 22 years younger than him.

Next came Wilson's magnum opus, *A Sketch of the Religious Sects of the Hindus*, published in two volumes; the first volume appeared in 1861. It was collected and edited by Reinhold Rost, the German orientalist who was a lecturer at St. Augustine's Missionary College, Canterbury. Rost knew many Indian languages, including Sanskrit, Pali, Tamil, Telugu and Urdu. The only drawback of this otherwise great book was the lack of consistency and uniformity in the transliteration of Indian names. This was because the author had to consult the many diverse manuscripts in different languages, including Persian, Sanskrit, Bengali and the different dialects of Hindi. Nevertheless, this book remains the crowning glory of Wilson's career.

It was generally acknowledged that apart from Colebrooke no European could be compared with Wilson when it came to his knowledge of the Sanskrit language. Wilson also researched and published on the matter of traditional Indian medical practices. A biographical notice in a report by the Royal Asiatic Society of Great Britain and Ireland in 1860 states:

> Neither official duties nor literary pursuits, nor these combined were sufficient for the active mind of our late director (while he was a resident at Calcutta). As a member of the society he joined with ardour in every scheme of public amusement and was, besides, the originator

> and promoter of many measures for the permanent improvement of the people among whom his lot was cast.

One of the lesser-known facets of Wilson's character was his passion for public education. He played an important part in the promotion of education among the local students, and devoted himself to developing the academic courses of Hindu College from the date of its establishment. According to Shumboo Dey in *Eminent Orientalists* published in 2000, 'Wilson was the first person who introduced the study of European science and English literature into the education of the native population whose knowledge of English had hitherto been confined to the qualification for situation of an office clerk.'

Though he was all for the introduction of the English language and European sciences in Indian schools, Wilson felt that it was neither feasible nor desirable to impose English as the medium of instruction in local schools. He was not in agreement with Macaulay's view that Western learning was superior and could only be taught through the medium of English. He staunchly opposed the proposal that English should be made the sole medium of instruction. This made Wilson unpopular amongst Englishmen and he was bitterly assailed for his views.

However, he was extremely popular amongst the locals, and had a reputation for being an ideal mentor. It is said of Wilson that no man was ever more willing to aid others in literary pursuits and many Sanskrit scholars have acknowledged their deep obligation to him. He was also good at encouraging even complete beginners, and spent many an hour in aiding people with their first efforts to learn Sanskrit.

After being appointed the Boden Professor of Sanskrit at Oxford in 1832, Wilson decided to depart for England the following January. The news about his impending departure cast a gloom over his large circle of friends and acquaintances in Calcutta. Over the years, Wilson had developed a strong bond with the local Sanskrit scholars, who felt that his departure would be a blow to the students and teachers of the Calcutta Sanskrit College.

On the eve of his departure, the pandits of the Sanskrit College met to bid him farewell. One of them dedicated a Sanskrit shloka to him, which loosely translated into English reads, as quoted in *Eminent Orientalists*: 'The Pandit swans, who dwell in this lake of the Sanskrit College, are deprived of their wings by the influence of malignant fate when thou art gone away for good.' This unique tribute softened Wilson's stern face and brought tears to his eyes.

Back in England, Wilson went directly to Oxford University and delivered his inaugural lecture in the summer of 1833. His topic was 'The General Principles of Sanskrit Grammar'. Wilson continued to promote the numerous branches of Indian learning, his zeal for mentoring remained undiminished. Beneath his writings and teaching flowed an undercurrent of enthusiasm that, despite a certain dryness of manner and baldness of style, often communicated itself to pupils or readers.

Initially, not many students registered for his class and his usual lectures were given only to a handful of students. Among them were E.B. Cowell and Monier Williams. The former would go on to become the principal of the Calcutta Sanskrit College in 1858, and in 1867, become the first professor of Sanskrit at Cambridge University. The latter would succeed his mentor and become the second Boden Professor of Sanskrit at Oxford.

Wilson lived with his family in Oxford for three years, before moving to London when he succeeded Sir Charles Wilkins as the librarian at East India House. He held this post until his death. During this period, Wilson also served as an examiner for Indian languages at the East India Company's training college at Haileybury and as director of the Royal Asiatic Society.

Among Horace Wilson's many publications was *Ariana Antiqua: A Descriptive Account of the Antiquities and Coins of Ancient Afghanistan*, released in 1841. This publication details the great discoveries of ancient coins and monuments in Punjab and Afghanistan. It was a landmark in this branch of studies. Wilson also released a new edition of *History of British India from 1805 to 1835*, in continuation of James Mill's *History (1844–1848)*. In this edition, as stated in *The English Cyclopædia* published in 1858, he 'endeavoured, by means of notes, to correct many of the errors into which Mill had fallen as a result of his prejudices against the Hindus and his ignorance of their language and literature'.

Another of Wilson's works was a voluminous glossary of judicial and revenue terms used in different parts of India. It had a lengthy title: *A Glossary of Judicial and Revenue Terms, and of Useful Words Occurring in Official Documents Relating to the Administration of the Government of British India from the Arabic, Persian, Hindustání, Sanskrit, Hindí, Bengálí, Uriya, Maráthi, Guzaráthí, Telugu, Karnáta, Tamil, Malayálam, and Other Languages.* He also contributed a number of articles on the religions, literature, coins, inscriptions and antiquities of India to the journals of various societies, especially to the Royal Asiatic Society.

Wilson's translation of the Rig Veda remains one of his most celebrated works. Based on the commentary of Sayana, an erudite pandit of South India, he began working on the project in 1850. However, Wilson died on 8 May 1860, before it could be completed. The work was finished by Cowell.

Another unfinished project of Wilson's was the cataloguing of the magnificent and unrivalled collection of Sanskrit manuscripts in the East India House library during his time as librarian there. Wilson had been a great collector of Sanskrit manuscripts, both Vedic and classical. Thanks to the extraordinary efforts put in by Wilson and his collaborator, Dr Theodor Goldstücker, more than 20,000 manuscripts were catalogued, including some priceless, rare originals. The most unique discovery was the original manuscript of *Manusmriti,* or 'Laws of Manu', which dates back to 100 CE.

While earlier orientalists were absorbed in the study of Vedic India, Wilson had been more interested in bringing to light the 'medieval India' or the 'post-Vedantic Indian history'. It was Wilson's firm belief that the only way to understand India's pre-Mughal past was to study ancient Hindu literature, poetry, coins and inscriptions. Kopf writes in his previously mentioned work that Wilson was fascinated by '"the perplexing labyrinth, those dark passages and cumbrous obstructions" that constituted the history of India between the Vedas and the rise of the Muslims'. Wilson's interest in this part of Indian history prepared the ground for the discovery of the Maurya and Gupta periods of India.

His successor to the Boden Chair of Sanskrit at Oxford, Williams, sums up Wilson's legacy in the following words stated in the 1894 book *Memorials of Old Haileybury College*:

> Wilson owed his celebrity to his boldness in entering upon investigations which no one had before attempted, to his excellence as a writer, to his faculty of lucid exposition, to the unusual versatility of his genius, including, as it did, poetical, dramatic, and musical powers of a high order, and perhaps, more than anything else, to his untiring industry and the wide range of his contributions to almost every brand of Oriental research.

8

SIR MONIER MONIER-WILLIAMS

Expounding Hinduism to the West

'The embodied spirit has a thousand heads,
A thousand eyes, a thousand feet, around
On every side enveloping the earth,
Yet filling space no larger than a span.
He is himself this very universe,
He is whatever is, has been, and shall be.
He is the lord of immortality…'

– Extract from a hymn in the Rig Veda[1]

December 1860

AFTER THE DEATH OF HORACE HAYMAN WILSON, THE FIRST Boden Professor of Sanskrit, an election was held to nominate

[1] From Monier-William's *Indian Wisdom; Or Examples of the Religious, Philosophical, and Ethical Doctrines of the Hindus* published in 1876.

his successor. It took place on 7 December 1860 in the Sheldonian Theatre, the official ceremonial hall of Oxford University. It had been an eventful election, which had taken on an atmosphere of a carnival. On that day, additional trains were provided to carry voters to Oxford from different parts of England.

The two contestants were Monier Monier-Williams, the orientalist who had taught Asian languages at the East India Company College from 1844, till the company rule in India ended in 1858, and Friedrich Max Müller, a German-born philosopher, philologist and orientalist. According to the *Times*, after a bitter campaign, the former won by a majority of over 220 votes, and was duly elected to the position of Boden Professor of Sanskrit at Oxford.

Unlike other British orientalists, Monier-Williams was born in India – in Bombay on 12 November 1819. He was the third of four sons born to Colonel Monier Williams, surveyor-general of the Bombay Presidency, and Hannah Sophia. Monier-Williams was sent to England in 1822 to study at a private school at Chelsea and Brighton. He later joined King's College School, London and graduated from Oxford University in March 1837. Later, in 1838–39, he studied Sanskrit at Balliol College, Oxford.

However, according to his submission to the members of the convocation of the University of Oxford quoted in *Religion in Victorian Britain* published in 1988, he had to leave when he received a nomination to a writership in the East India Company's civil service in November 1839. He passed his examination at the East India House in December. He then left Oxford and went into residence at the East India

Company's college, Haileybury, in January 1840, where he did well in almost all the chief Oriental subjects.

As he was preparing to leave England to take up his assignment in India, he got the tragic news that his younger brother had been killed during the Siege of Kahun in Sindh. This episode entirely changed the course of his career. His mother pleaded with him to not leave the country, leading to Monier-Williams turning down the Indian appointment. He returned to Oxford and joined the University College in May 1841.

Early in life, Monier-Williams had shown great linguistic prowess. Thus, it was not surprising that he took up Sanskrit at Oxford. He had the good fortune of studying under the renowned Sanskrit scholar, Horace Hayman Wilson. In 1843, Monier-Williams became a Boden Sanskrit scholar at Oxford, and in the following year he joined the teaching staff at Haileybury as professor of Sanskrit, Persian and Hindustani. He also taught Bengali and Telugu.

In 1848, while still at Haileybury, he married Julia, with whom he was to have six sons and a daughter. He remained at Haileybury for 15 years, until the college was closed following the Indian Rebellion of 1857. The teaching staff were pensioned off the following year. Thus, Monier-Williams was looking for a job when a vacancy for the prestigious position of Boden Professor of Sanskrit opened up after the death of his mentor Wilson in 1860.

Interestingly, back when Wilson became the first Boden Professor in 1831, he had expressed his preference for Monier-Williams as his successor. However, there was another claimant for the chair: the famous German philosopher, Max Müller. Monier-Williams had not expected that he would have such a powerful rival to contend with. The fight for the position became extremely challenging as well as acrimonious. The elections were widely publicized and became a media carnival, with newspapers and journals jumping into the fray. Campaigners from both sides advertised in the papers and circulated manifestos backing their chosen candidate.

But soon it became evident to everyone that Monier-Williams was gaining popularity. It was more for his religious views rather than his scholarship. As per *Religion*, the *Record,* an evangelical publication, stated that though Müller's works were familiar to people interested in literature, 'they have destroyed confidence in his religious opinions'. Monier-Williams was being portrayed as a man of sincere piety and one who is likely 'to promote the ultimate object which the founder of the Professorship had in view'.

Other papers eulogized Monier-Williams both for his religious views and his philosophical knowledge of the Vedic literature. Even those who admitted that Monier-Williams was not as brilliant a scholar as Müller supported his candidature, citing the fact that he had first-hand knowledge about India, whereas Müller had never visited India.

A newspaper that was strongly in support of Müller was the *Times.* In its editorial on 29 October 1860, Müller was described as 'nothing more nor less than the best Sanscrit scholar in the world'. The editorial compared the 1860 election with the one in 1832, when there had also been a choice between the best scholar (Wilson) and a good scholar

(William Hodge Mill), 'who was held to have made the most Christian use of the gift'. It pointed out that in 1832, the better scholar had won.

However, there were some who considered Monier-Williams the better scholar of the two. Interestingly, amongst them was an Indian: Nishi Kanta Chattopadhyay, a renowned Bengali scholar who was the first Indian to get a Ph.D from a European university, had met both the candidates, and felt that Monier-Williams was a shade above Müller when it came to scholarship.

As the tempo of election progressed, the focus shifted to the nationality rather than the scholarship of the candidates. A majority of the publications focused negatively on the fact that Müller was a German. London newspaper the *Homeward Mail* asked its readers whether they wanted 'a stranger and a foreigner' to win, or 'one of your own body'. And the *Morning Herald* went to the extent of declaring it 'a question of national interest'. According to the religious historian Gwilym Beckerlegge in *Religion*, 'voting for the Boden Chair was increasingly taking on the appearance of being a test of patriotism.'

After the results were declared, in a letter found in *Life and Letters* published in 1902, Müller blamed his defeat on 'calumnious falsehood and vulgar electioneering tactics' that made his German background and the general impression that he held nonconformist religious views work against him. Much later, Monier-Williams admitted in his unpublished autobiography that he had been 'favoured by circumstances', and also acknowledged that the main reason for his victory in the election was that he was considered politically and religiously conservative, as opposed to Müller, who was viewed as a bit of a maverick.

Soon after assuming the position of Boden Professor, Monier-Williams repaid the confidence of his supporters by declaring that the conversion of India to the Christian religion should be one of the aims of oriental scholarship. He further emphasized his views on the role of the position by giving his inaugural lecture on the topic of 'The Study of Sanskrit in Relation to Missionary Work'. This was in keeping with the wishes of Boden himself.

How serious was Monier-Williams's advocacy of the missionary enterprise in India? Whether he really meant it or it was said to keep his supporters happy is a matter of dispute amongst scholars. Regardless, there is no disagreement on his momentous contributions to the cause of Sanskrit studies.

One of Monier-Williams's most significant achievements in this field was the creation of the Indian Institute in Oxford. A long-held dream of his had been to create an association at Oxford that would be a focal point for the dissemination of correct information about Indian literature and culture. He had been planning the project right from the early 1870s. It finally took shape when he formally proposed the foundation of an Indian Institute at a congregation at Oxford on 13 May 1875.

It was dedicated not only to learning the literature of India, but also to provide a 'stable study environment for both Indian Civil Service (ICS) probationers and Indian students' at Oxford. Besides promoting the welfare of Indians in Oxford, it would disseminate general knowledge of India among those studying at Oxford, some of whom might go on to exercise control over India's destiny in the British Parliament.

The building was to include a library with a wide collection of books and newspapers, a reading room, lecture rooms and a museum. As per 'History of the Old Indian Institute', Monier-Williams's concept was, in his own words, to 'present to the eye a typical collection of facts, illustrations and examples which...will give a concise synopsis of India – of the country and its material products – of the people and their moral condition.'

An ambitious enterprise like this required generous funding, and Monier-Williams decided to travel to India to seek aid for the institute. He undertook three journeys to India – in 1875, 1876 and 1883 – to enlist the aid of educated Indians and some of the native princes in his scheme. These were the only occasions when he visited India. His efforts were rewarded with success, and he could raise nearly £34,000 from subscribers in India and the United Kingdom for the institute.

Besides large contributions from the Indian princes, Monier-Williams also received generous donations from Queen Victoria and the Prince of Wales. One of the most avid supporters of the proposal for the Indian Institute was Benjamin Jowett, master of Balliol College and later vice-chancellor of Oxford, who was particularly concerned with university reform and was consulted on reforms to the Indian Civil Service. The foundation stone of the Indian Institute was laid on 2 May 1883 by the Prince of Wales. The building was constructed in three phases. The first phase was completed in 1884, and was inaugurated on 14 October of that year by Jowett in the presence of the Marquis of Salisbury.

The last phase was finished in 1896 and the building was officially declared open by Lord George Hamilton, secretary of state for India. There is no doubt that it was Monier-Williams's sheer perseverance, fortitude and single-minded devotion that could bring this ambitious project to completion.

This was Monier-Williams's lasting memorial in Oxford, not only in lifeless stone, but also in the living influence of generations of Indian students. His students used to affectionately refer to him as *munivar* or 'great sage'. Monier-Williams had the good fortune of seeing in his lifetime the Indian Institute become a famous centre of enquiry and research for scholars interested in India. He subsequently presented his large and priceless collection of about 3,000 oriental manuscripts and books to the library of the Indian Institute.

The institute was an extension of Monier Monier-Williams's tremendous admiration for the Sanskrit language, which, according to his words in *Indian Wisdom,* was 'accepted and revered by all adherents of Hinduism alike, however diverse in race, dialect, rank and creed...' He declared Sanskrit literature to be 'the repository of Veda, or "knowledge" in its widest sense; the vehicle of Hindu theology, philosophy, law, and mythology; the one guide to the intricacies and the contradictions of Hinduism ; the one bond of sympathy, which, like an electric chain, connects Hindus of opposite characters in every district of India.'

Monier-Williams's great admiration of Hindu literature is evident from many of his observations, especially in *Indian*

Wisdom. He noted that there are many passages in the Ramayana and Mahabharata 'which for beauty of description cannot be surpassed by anything in Homer' and the diction was 'more polished, regular, and cultivated and the language altogether in a more advanced stage of development than that of Homer.' He goes on to say, the Ramayana is undoubtedly one of the greatest treasure in Sanskrit literature. 'The classical purity, clearness and simplicity of its style, the exquisite touches of true poetic feeing with which it abounds....' Monier-Williams ranks it 'among the most beautiful compositions that appeared at any period or any country.'

Monier-Williams differed from other orientalists of his time as his focus was almost exclusively on the study of the later period rather than the oldest phase of Indian literature. He wanted to increase the knowledge of Indian religions in Britain. An insatiable writer, he translated a large number of Sanskrit literary works, beginning with a collection of Kalidasa's plays, titled *Vikramorvasi*, published in 1849. It was followed by *Sakuntala* in 1853 and the *Nalopakhyana, or Episode of Nala* from the Mahabharata in 1879. He also wrote some Hindustani manuals, among which were *An Easy Introduction to the Study of Hindustani Words*, published in 1858, and *A Practical Hindústání Grammar*, published in 1862.

Monier-Williams wrote copiously on Hinduism.As quoted in Saral Jhingran's *Aspects of Hindu Morality*, he describes Hinduism as a 'huge polygon or irregular multilateral figure' that was unified by Sanskrit literature. According to him, 'no description of Hinduism can be exhaustive which does not touch on almost every religious and philosophical idea that the world has ever known.' His other publications include *Indian Wisdom: With a Brief History of the Chief Departments of Sanskrit Literature and Some Account of the Past and Present Condition of India, Moral and Intellectual; Hinduism; Modern India and the Indians, Religious Life and Thought in India, Buddhism,* and *Brahmanism.* Most of these books enjoyed a great deal of popularity.

Right from the time he had been teaching Sanskrit at Haileybury, Monier-Williams had been planning a 'etymologically and philologically arranged Sanskrit-English dictionary'. He firmly believed that, as mentioned in the dictionary,

> [T]he primary object of a Sanskrit dictionary should be to exhibit, by a lucid etymological arrangement, the structure of a language which, as most people know, is not only the elder sister of Greek, but the best guide to the structure of Greek, as well as of every other member of the Aryan or Indo-European family. A language, in short which is the very keystone of the science of comparative philology.

The dictionary was finally published in 1872 under the title *A Sanskrit-English Dictionary: Etymologically and Philologically Arranged with Special Reference to Cognate Indo-European Languages.* It was widely hailed as a brilliant work of scholarship and as an essential reference book for Sanskrit scholars.

Monier-Williams was knighted in 1876 and was made Knight Commander of the Order of the Indian Empire in 1887. Soon after, he adopted his given name of Monier as an additional surname and became known as Sir Monier

Monier-Williams. By then his health had deteriorated and he retired from teaching that year. After giving up his residence in the university, he began spending the winter months in southern France every year.

Monier-Williams devoted the last years of his life to the completion of the second edition of his *Sanskrit-English Dictionary*. Since the publication of the first version of this dictionary, there had been a great deal of progress in Sanskrit scholarship and a large number of new words needed to be included. Monier-Williams realized that with so much text to be integrated, the entire dictionary would have to be rewritten.

About 60,000 new Sanskrit words were included in the second edition, and references and quotations for the use and specific meaning of every word in different Vedic literature texts were added. The layout of the dictionary was made clearer and easier to use. With the help of assistants and other workers, this mammoth undertaking was completed by Monier-Williams in April 1899. He gave the final touches to this work just a few days before his death.

The revised *Sanskrit-English Dictionary* was published within a month of his death, with the following postscript added by his son, M.F. Monier-Williams:

> This Dictionary, to which my father devoted so many years of labour, was completed by him a few days before his death, which took place at Cannes, in the south of France, on April 11, 1899. It had been his hope to see this work published shortly after his return to England. Although this desire was not granted, it was a satisfaction to him to know that the last revise had received his final corrections, and

that the book would be issued from the University Press within a few weeks of his death.
May 4, 1899
M.F. Monier-Williams

Monier Monier-Williams died at Cannes on 11 April 1899, and his remains were brought back to England and interred in the village churchyard at Chessington, Surrey.

9

FREDERIC SALMON GROWSE

Translating the Living Faith of India

'So much irreparable damage has been done in past years from simple ignorance as to the value of ancient architectural remains, that I have been careful to describe in full every building in the district which possesses the slightest historical or artistic interest. […] I dwell at considerable length on the legends connected with the deified Krishna, the tutelary divinity of the district: because… they have materially affected the course of local history and are still household words, to which allusion is constantly made in conversation, either to animate a description or to enforce an argument.'

– Fredric Salmon Growse in *Mathurá: A District Memoir*, 1882

1883, Mathura

AT THE SUNRISE HOUR, THE BANKS OF THE YAMUNA WERE ALREADY crowded with pilgrims and worshippers. The bare-chested men, the women draped in bright cotton sarees, mendicants in loincloths, priests in saffron and the widows in white; the scene rarely varied.

Among the crowd was an Englishman, whom the locals of Mathura knew as a Hindi scholar who spoke to them in their local dialect; a man who had a penchant for wandering amidst the ruins of the past. He was Frederic Salmon Growse, the collector and district magistrate of Mathura in the North Western Provinces (now Uttar Pradesh), a much loved and respected figure.

By then, he was already known as an idealist, researcher and archaeologist who loved India. Indians spoke of him with awe and reverence, and referred to him as 'Mahatma Growse'. They appreciated him for translating the *Ramcharitmanas* into English from Awadhi so that the world could learn about this holy book.

Frederic Salmon Growse, the son of Robert Growse, was born in 1836 at Bildeston, Suffolk. He was educated at Oriel College and Queen's College, Oxford, where he earned a master's degree. He came to India after he passed the competitive examination for the Indian Civil Service in 1859. The following year, he joined the Bengal Civil Services as an assistant collector at Mainpuri. In 1871, Growse was posted to the North-Western Provinces as a joint magistrate in Mathura.

Growse was an extraordinary officer and left his mark at each of the stations where he was posted. He firmly believed that it was of utmost importance to have an intimate knowledge of the habits, views, and thinking of the local people for a sympathetic administrator. His attitude was in sharp contrast to other officers posted to India, who, in Growse's words from his 1884 publication *Bulandshahr*, made no secret of their 'contempt for the race they are called upon to rule'. Growse never lost sight of the fact that it would create discontent if English officers failed to understand the locals and their interests.

Keeping this in mind, he devoted himself to studying the local languages and literature early on in his career. This was done more as a labour of love than from a sense of duty. He believed that real appreciation of the people of another culture began with the understanding of their psyche and their language.

From the moment he landed in Mathura, Growse began burning the midnight oil to learn Hindi. He soon become an ardent defender of the purity of the Hindi language and opposed the official language of Hindustani, which was a mixture of Hindi and Urdu. He felt so strongly on this subject that he even got into a disagreement with John Beames, a fellow British officer who was known for his pioneering work *Comparative Grammar of the Aryan Languages of India* published in three volumes from 1872–79.

Of all his accomplishments in India, the one that earned Growse the enduring love of the people of Mathura was his English translation of Tulsidas's magnum opus, *Ramcharitmanas,* considered as one of the greatest works of Hindi literature. Growse knew that the *Ramcharitmanas* was to the people of the North-Western Provinces what the Bible was for the Christians. His personal observation, quoted by R.C. Prasad in the edited version of the book published in 1987, was that 'the book (Ramcharitmanas) is in everyone's hands, from the court to the cottage, and is read, or heard, or appreciated alike by every class of the Hindu community, whether high or low, rich or poor, young or old.'

He began the onerous task of translating the *Ramcharitmanas* in 1883. The task was rendered even more complex as the epic had been written in Awadhi, which was a local dialect of Hindi. Growse noted in the preface of his book that, 'No one...can fully appreciate the amount of thought that has to be expended on almost every sentence before the peculiarities of Oriental expression can be adapted to the requirements of English idiom.' He never lost sight of the fact that without the most subtle handling, it would be impossible to avoid 'either a sacrifice of accuracy in the letter or a misrepresentation of the spirit'.

His English version was titled *Ramayana of Tulsīdāsa*, and in his introduction he considered it to be 'the best and most trustworthy guide to the popular living faith of the Hindu race at the present day'. Growse did not expect that his work would be so hugely successful. However, the work received accolades not just for its precision and accuracy but also for its consistently noble and elevated tone.

According Prasad, who wrote the preface to the second edition of the book, 'Growse was familiar with the deepest stratum of art—the images of myth, religious and poetic... Growse's translation answers much the same cravings of imagination and feeling as the original Hindi *Rāmāyana*... in which the tradition of oral poetry blends harmoniously with that of the literary epic.'

However, Growse's claim to fame does not rest on the Ramayana alone. He is also remembered for his pioneering work in discovering and preserving numerous antiquities in and around Mathura, and for his vast research and documentation of Mathura and Vrindavan. He was one of the early explorers of Mathura district, often seen walking around ruins in the region. The sight of this sparely built Englishman hanging around the ancient ruins of Mathura in faded trousers and buff-coloured solar topee had become familiar to the locals.

Mathura was an archaeologist's paradise, and it reawakened the classicist in Growse. Soon after his arrival in the district, Growse began to spend gruelling hours excavating the area in and around the district of Mathura, rescuing priceless artefacts. Though many of his scholarly articles on his archaeological discoveries were published in academic journals, Growse felt that his work was far from done. He wanted to write a book documenting the history and culture of Mathura in detail. For a book of that magnitude, he needed to collect more information about the district, the people, their attitude and their way of life. Thus began his voyage for the discovery of India.

It began with his investigation into the Krishna *Janmasthan*, or Keshava Deva Temple. It was a site that had been venerated as the birthplace of Lord Krishna for generations. Growse was aware that the Shahi-Eidgah, the red sandstone mosque occupying the same location, was built by the Mughal emperor Aurangzeb. However, very few people knew that the Keshava Deva temple had been built on the site where centuries ago had existed Yasa Vihara, a large Buddhist monastery.

It was Sir Alexander Cunningham, the pioneer of Indian archaeology, who first suggested that Yasa Vihara dated back to the Kushana period. The inscriptions found at the site confirmed that it was in existence even in days of the Gupta Empire. Growse's excavations of ancient mounds in and around Mathura further established Cunningham's theory. Amongst the many scattered artefacts was a sculpture of Kubera, the king of the Yakshas. According to Hindu, Jain and Buddhist texts, this semi-divine being is the guardian of the treasures of the earth.

In Pali Khera, a site in Mathura, Growse unearthed a part of the world-famous 'bacchanalian' group of sculptures. It proved to be a veritable goldmine as he dug up many sculptural gems, including a second bacchanalian group. More importantly, he found a statue of Parshvanatha, the 23rd *Tirthankara*, or spiritual teacher, of Jainism, who lived from 872 to 772 BCE.

Growse also extracted a number of basement stones at Pali Khera suggesting the presence of a much older shrine at the same site. These sculptural remains show that though Mathura is revered as the birthplace of Lord Krishna, there is ample evidence that it was also a centre for the Buddhist and Jain devotees, and that the city was a religious hub even before the arrival of the Kushanas in the first century BCE.

It came as a surprise to Growse that many remains of railings and gateways which once graced the shrines of Mathura bore a startling similarity to the famous Buddhist monuments at Bharhut and Sanchi in Madhya Pradesh. Among the artefacts dug out was a colossal Buddha head and an inscribed pedestal belonging to the 33rd year of the reign of the Kushana king Huvishka, who ruled from 140 to 183 CE. Growse sent all these artefacts to the Lucknow museum and wrote several papers on his finds in the 'Journal of the Asiatic Society of Bengal' as well as other leading research journals.

Growse was highly disconcerted by the apathetic attitude then prevalent towards priceless antiquities, many going back to the first and second century CE. He was particularly flabbergasted to find stone inscriptions from the reign of Huvishka set in a PWD (Public Works Department) culvert, and another one studded in the gate of the tehsil! Growse wasted no time in retrieving these along with a Naga figure from Kukargaon, and arranged for them to be conserved.

He cared for preserving precious artefacts as much as he liked excavating them. It was not as if antiquarian remains had not been unearthed earlier, but before he came on the scene, none had bothered to preserve them, at least not locally. The fate of these ancient relics depended upon the mercy of the excavator or the officer interested in them. Once in a while, they were sent to Lucknow or the Indian Museum at Calcutta.

In 1874, Growse decided to do something about the unauthorized removal of these precious relics, and set out measures to stop the outflow of antiques from the district. He strongly believed that these precious objects needed to be housed in an architectural and antiquarian museum within the district. With this in mind, he selected an old building near the civil courts, originally intended as a rest house, as the site for the proposed museum.

The museum however remained a sculptural shed and was not opened to the members of the public for many years. Finally, in 1933, it was moved to a new building specifically constructed for the purpose. From a small nucleus, the Mathura museum today boasts of a unique collection of Mauryan, Sunga, Kushana, Jain and Brahmanical artefacts, which had all been discovered in and around Mathura. It remains an enduring memorial to the artistic and architectural genius of Growse.

Another memorable achievement of Growse was the planning and erection of a Catholic chapel in Mathura. Perhaps for the first time in India, an attempt was made to blend local art with Christian architecture. The cost of building the chapel was covered entirely through private donations, of which Growse contributed the lion's share. Today, it stands as a monument to his rare artistic taste and architectural skill. In the words of Growse from his 1874 book *Mathurá*, 'the chapel is intended as a protest against the standard plans and other stereotyped conventionalities of the Public Works Department.'

Around that time, a popular book was fellow British officer Sir W.W. Hunter's pioneering work *The Annals of Rural Bengal,* published in 1868. Taking its cue from these chronicles, the government of the North-Western Provinces too decided to publish a series of local memoirs of its districts. Growse's passion for archaeology, his scholarly bent of mind and, most importantly, his love and intimate knowledge of his subject made him the most fitting candidate for the onerous task of chronicling all aspects of Vrindavan and Mathura of that period.

However, good libraries did not exist outside the presidency towns. This made the task all the more difficult for Growse. He gathered his material not just from what he had gleaned from his excavations, but also from folklores, local legends, manners and customs. By dint of extensive research and indefatigable industry, he was able to put together minute details about Mathura and its environs. They were published as *Mathura: A District Memoir* in 1874.

The book was hailed as a unique encyclopaedia and dictionary on Mathura and Vrindavan. So thorough was the documentation that even today, after more than a century since publication, it stands out as the most celebrated monograph that has been written on an Indian district. The memoir was widely commended and one cannot but agree with the review that said a book of this magnitude could only be written by a person inspired by a genuine love for India and the Indian people.

In 1880, a new enlarged edition with beautiful photographs was published; but by then Growse had been moved out of his beloved Mathura against his will. His employers were rather harsh on him and he was transferred to Bulandshahr.

Nevertheless, Growse did not give up his scholastic pursuit. His area of research shifted to Bulandshahr district, which had a sizeable Muslim population. His book, *Bulandshahr; Or, Sketches of an Indian District: Social, Historical and Architectural* came out in 1884. The title page of this book carries the epigraph from J.R. Seeley, set in small capitals: 'OUR WESTERN CIVILIZATION IS PERHAPS NOT ABSOLUTELY THE GLORIOUS THING WE LIKE TO IMAGINE IT.'

Growse retired in 1890 and returned to England. He settled down in Haslemere, Surrey, where he died of pulmonary tuberculosis on 18 May 1893. The most inexplicable as well as tragic aspect of his life is that though he had been a highly respected personality in India, and had been given the honour of 'Companion of Indian Empire', Growse was unsung in his native land. He fell out of favour with his compatriots because of his deep empathy with the 'natives', the very same reason that had made him a savant amongst the people of Mathura. Growse's name does not even figure in the list of notable former inhabitants of Haslemere.

However, in India he left behind an outstanding legacy as a scholar, litterateur, translator and compiler, and also for his pioneering work in archaeology, excavation and preservation of priceless artefacts. Growse would not have had the success he achieved had he not treated India as his home. In the preface of *Bulandshahr,* he wrote:

> My own career, now almost at an end... I have only known three districts; Mainpuri as an Assistant, Mathura as Joint Magistrate, and Bulandshahr as Collector. Each for the time being was my home, in which all my interests were centred, and in each I have left a permanent record of my connection with the place.

The English weekly newspaper the *Tablet* paid a tribute to Growse, as found in *Mathurá*:

> We wish there were more civil servants like Mr. Growse, with eyes open to see and intellects cultivated to appreciate the marvels of which the country where their sphere of duty lies... Unhappily, Indian 'civilians' are as a class, Philistine to their heart's core... It is a very exceptional thing for them to possess a real knowledge of the colloquial vernacular...they know next to nothing really of the habits, standpoints, and modes of thought of the people. They do not think it is worth knowing. Contempt for the race they are called upon to rule is too often the dominant feeling in the awkward, cold, pig-headed and narrowminded young Englishmen who go out to India, from an English

> university... It is a feeling which is absolutely fatal to any intelligent appreciation of Hindu or Muhammadan art or literature.

Frederic Salmon Growse was an honourable exception. To further quote the Tablet, he brought an 'eye for all he saw and brought too, no inconsiderable literary faculty to describe what he saw.' He truly loved India and its people.

10

SIR GEORGE ABRAHAM GRIERSON

A Linguist Par Excellence

'As compiler of many grammars of known and unknown languages (of India), editor and translator of many Middle and Modern Indo-Aryan texts, he (Grierson) had more than any other contributed to our knowledge of the innumerable languages and dialects of India.'

– A tribute to George Abraham Grierson
on his 85th birthday[1]

8 May 1928, London

A LAVISH LUNCHEON WAS BEING HOSTED BY THE ROYAL ASIATIC Society of Great Britain and Ireland at the opulent Criterion Restaurant in London. Amongst the approximately 90 guests was a very distinguished-looking gentleman in his late

---

[1] From *Indian and Iranian Studies* by R.L. Turner and H.W. Bailey published in 1936.

seventies. His round-rimmed spectacles and flowing grey beard added to his scholarly appearance. The man was Sir George Abraham Grierson of the Indian Civil Service, and the party was being held to celebrate the publication of his magnum opus, *The Linguistic Survey of India.* The project had been started in 1898 and it had taken him 30 years to finish.

Grierson accepted the accolades at the party with the following words, recorded at the end of the *Survey*: 'I lay these volumes as an offering before India that was long my home and that has itself had home in my heart for more than half a century. Throughout my active life among the people who I soon learned to love…' How did his love affair with India begin?

George Abraham Grierson was born on 7 January 1851 in Glenageary, Dublin, in Ireland. He was the eldest son of a barrister, George, and Isabella. Interestingly, both his father and grandfather were named George Grierson, and were well-known printers to the Royal Family of England.

Grierson studied at St. Bees School and Trinity College, Dublin. It was in Trinity that he met Professor Robert Atkinson, a legendary teacher of Romance languages. The professor had an incredible aptitude for languages and also taught Arabic, Sanskrit, Tamil and Telugu, among others. Meeting Atkinson was a defining moment in Grierson's life. 'It was to me a memorable day,' he recalls in the concluding remarks of the *Survey*, 'when in 1868 my honoured teacher Professor Robert Atkinson introduced me to the Sanskrit alphabet'.

Thus, inspired by Atkinson, young George Abraham took up the study of Sanskrit and Hindi at Trinity College, Dublin. And his extraordinary language skills were demonstrated when, as an undergraduate, he walked away with the prizes for both Sanskrit and Hindi. Ultimately, it was this profound fascination with Indian languages that played a major role in his career and took him to the forefront of the list of Orient scholars.

Grierson qualified for the Indian Civil Service in 1871 and arrived in India in 1873. Just before leaving for India, he went to bid farewell to his teacher. Atkinson's advice to him was to take on the task of 'conducting a linguistic survey of India'. Grierson accepted. However, more than 20 years would pass before 'the opportunity and the privilege of conducting the linguistic survey' would come his way.

During those years, he prepared for the colossal task he had pledged to undertake. Grierson confirms in his introduction to the *Survey* that

> [P]ersonally these years of preparation were by no means without profit. I have been granted a vision of a magnificent literature enshrining the thoughts of great men from generation to generation through three thousand years. I have been able to stroll through enchanted gardens of poesy beginning with the happy carefree hymns of the Vedas, continuing through great epics, through the magic of Indian drama and the consummate world witchery of Kalidasa...

And all through this time, Robert Atkinson's injunction to conduct a linguistic survey of India was ever present in his mind.

When Grierson arrived in India, the Bengal Presidency included present-day Bengal, Bihar and Orissa. He began his career in 1873 as subdivisional officer at Madhubani,

Darbhanga in present-day Bihar at 22. It was during this posting that his fascination for India started to take shape, and he began spending all his free time reading the ancient Indian classics.

His interest in philology and linguistics led him to study the languages and folklore of India, and gradually he expanded his field of study to include the behavioural pattern of the local people and how it was influenced by their customs, traditions and way of life.

In 1880, Grierson was posted as inspector of schools. The same year he married Lucy Elizabeth Jean, but did not slow down his work. His original tour diaries bear testimony to his arduous routine. Grierson continued serving in a series of government posts until 1898. By the time he took charge as magistrate and collector at Patna, he was delving deep into the stories, legends, proverbs and anecdotes of Bihar, all narrated verbally by the local people.

What made Grierson's study unique was that he photographed the people he interviewed. He was a keen photographer and captured his interactions with the people on his camera. The sight of the camera fascinated and sometimes alarmed the people of the district, who had never seen one before. 'The camera was looked upon as a fearful engine of destruction,' recalled Grierson in the introduction to his book mentioned below. 'Sometimes half an hour had been wasted in futile diplomacy to persuade an old lady to allow the lens to be pointed at her.'

In a few years' time he had gathered enough information and photographs to write one of his most important tomes. His 592-page illustrated volume was published in 1885 under the protracted title *Bihār Peasant Life: Being a Discursive Catalogue of the Surroundings of the People of that Province: with Many Illustrations from Photographs Taken by the Author.* The book was not only a storehouse of information on linguistics, art and culture of the people but also shed light on the life of the poor smallholders, agricultural labourers, farming methods, and the beliefs and superstitions of the peasants of Bihar.

Another unique feature of the book was that all the information was presented not in a narrative form but in simple words and phrases, proverbs and sayings used in daily life by the peasants. It was the first work of its kind where words and expressions from all over the district were used to reflect the pain and problems of the rural world, and the hard life of the peasantry. The book showcased Grierson's profound insight into the life of the peasants of Bihar, and by 1887 his papers, reviews and books began to appear all over the world.

Grierson was an avid writer, and also authored several other books during that period. The books were about the language spoken in Madhubani, and included *Seven Grammars of the Dialects and Subdialects of the Bihári Language Spoken in Bihár, An Introduction to the Maithilí Language of North Bihár,* and *A Handbook to the Kaithi Character.* He also wrote *The Modern Vernacular Literature of Hindustan,* with a catalogue of 952 authors and writings in the dialects from Rajasthan to the borders of Bengal.

Grierson was painstakingly methodical in his work and spared no pains to maintain the greatest accuracy possible. Siddhartha Sen notes in his essay 'George Abraham Grierson,

1851-1941' that each anecdote or story was written out in local script before being translated into English. He further quotes Grierson:

> When the work began to assume shape, it was carefully compared with every available book of reference, and where discrepancies occurred, they were either reconciled or explained. Finally, the proof sheets have been circulated to all the Bihār districts, and have been again checked on the spot by competent observers, different from the original persons who collected the materials on which the book was founded.

In 1886, Grierson attended the International Congress of Orientalists in Vienna as a delegate of the Royal Asiatic Society. There, he mooted the idea of a formal linguistic survey of India. As a result, a resolution was passed urging the Indian colonial government to undertake a deliberate systematic survey of the languages of India. At the time, even the total number of Indian languages was not known. The estimate varied from anything between 20 to 250!

The project was sanctioned in 1894, and four years later, Grierson was put on special duty as editor. The undertaking involved the linguistic survey of 224 million out of a population of 294 million (Madras and the states of Hyderabad and Mysore were excluded from the survey). According to Dr Siddhartha Sen of the school of mathematics at Trinity College, the task required an incredible amount of planning as the country had to be divided into subdivisions and instructions sent to each district officer. It was decided that the survey would be done in three parts: (i) A standard passage (for comparison) was to be translated into every known dialect and subdialect spoken in the areas covered by the operation; (ii) A representative narrative or prose passage was to be locally selected and translated; (iii) A standard list of 241 words and test sentences were to be translated. These were test sentences originally drawn up in 1866 for the Asiatic Society of Bengal by Sir George Campbell.

The standard passage selected for translation was the parable of the Prodigal Son. Since the majority of those being approached in the survey were not expected to be familiar with this parable, it was essential to produce, as a preliminary step, specimen translations of the parable in various Indian languages. This was done for 65 languages by 1897.

With the cooperation of local officials, Grierson made a first list of all the known languages and dialects within the areas to be covered by the survey. He started his survey with the most difficult languages: the Indo-Chinese languages related to the languages of Assam, eastern Bengal and upper Burma.

One of the unique aspects about the study was the idea of recording dialects and languages by gramophone. Gramophone recordings were made of stories, songs and poems in different dialects and languages, such as those spoken by aboriginal tribes of Chhota Nagpur and the Santhal Parganas (in present-day Jharkhand). These recordings are of great historical and philological value. In the words of Grierson, mentioned in the preface of *Gramophone Records of the Languages and Dialects of Madras Presidency*, 'besides the great interest that such records would arouse by enabling the languages to be heard spoken by members of the tribe concerned, they would be useful to students of languages, and to phoneticians, who would thus be put in the possession of the actual sounds used in each language'.

Some unexpected and amusing predicaments came up during the survey. After the forms had been returned, it was time to analyse the answers. Though each officer knew the main language of their particular district, they would often come upon a tiny community speaking a dialect that no one was familiar with. One example was a Himalayan district in which the main language was Indo-Aryan, but in the district, there was a small colony, originally from Tibet, which had retained its own language. Grierson wrote in the *Survey*, 'No official knew the language and the discussion with them was carried through the medium of a lingua franca.' Even the name of the language was not known. When the district officer entered the name of this language in his form, it was noticed that the name was not one or two words but 'was a solemn process of weird monosyllables wandering right across the page'!

Neither Grierson nor his Tibetan friends could make anything out of it. After all his endeavours to identify the name of the language failed, he wrote to the district officer. It was only after that did they understand 'the monosyllabic procession was not the name of a language but was the local way of saying "I don't understand what you are driving at in broken Tibetan!"'

Another unexpected difficulty was the naming of dialects. Very often, Grierson notes in the survey, the average villager did not know that 'he has been speaking with anything that has a name attached to it. He can put a name to a language spoken by somebody 50 miles off' but was at a loss when asked about his own. Grierson came to the conclusion that most dialect names are not those given by the speakers but those given by the neighbours.

An obituary of his life published in 1942, by Indologist Frederick William Thomas and Indian language philologist Sir Ralph Lilley Turner, mentions that in 1900, Grierson moved back to England 'for convenience of consulting European libraries and scholars'. By 1903, most of the data had come in. He retired from the Indian Civil Service and began editing the enormous amount of material gathered. Grierson collaborated with the Norwegian linguist Sten Konow on Tibetan languages.

Grierson worked from his home in Camberley, Surrey, called Rathfarnham. He refused to accept emoluments beyond his ordinary pension, and did away with his office and staff. The final volume of the 19 volumes of the linguistic survey of India appeared in May 1928.

The survey ran to 8,000 pages and documented information on 179 languages and 544 dialects. Four separate families of languages were recognized: Austro-Asiatic, Sino-Tibetan, Dravidian and Aryan. Grierson had an obsession for accuracy and made sure that the printed version was compared three times with the manuscript.

Grierson's work was marked by his modesty of assertion and his constant readiness to share his researches with other enquirers, even before he was ready to publish the result. In the previously mentioned obituary, Turner and Thomas referred to the publication as 'a great imperial museum, representing and systematically classifying the linguistic botany of India'.

In India, Grierson had inspired deep admiration and love. One of them was W.G. Archer, a British civil servant and art historian who had served in Bihar from 1931 to around 1947 and worked in Madhubani, almost fifty years after Grierson. Archer was pleasantly surprised to find Grierson's name was still on the lips of the people of the region. William Archer mentions in his memoirs – written in partnership with his wife, Dr Mildred Archer – *India Served and Observed*, that the main market of the town was named after Grierson but was mispronounced by the locals.

Archer wrote to Sir Grierson that the market named after him still existed, but was being pronounced 'Gilesanganj'. Prompt came the great linguist's reply that the reason for the 'mispronunciation' was that the people of Bihar pronounced every 'r' as 'l'. He illustrated his point by giving the example of the Ganges valley inscriptions written by the great emperor Ashoka in 250 BCE. Grierson pointed out that in these inscriptions the word 'laja' was written in place of 'raja'. Ashoka is an apt case in point as the emperor lived in Patna, hence he was technically a Bihari!

On 7 January 1936, on the occasion of his 85th birthday, Grierson was presented with a volume of *Indian and Iranian Studies*, to which 52 scholars from all parts of the world had contributed. Professor R.L. Turner, one of the editors of the book, made the presentation. According to a report in the *Times*, the introductory address described Sir George Grierson as

> [M]ore worthily upholding the great tradition of (Sir) William Jones than any Englishman of this age. The long list of his publications, extending over nearly sixty years,

> bore witness to the boundless energy and enthusiasm and to the firmness of spirit which, held undeviating on the path he had chosen, had triumphed over every difficulty of circumstances.

Grierson never stopped writing. The completion of the survey took him 30 years! At the end Grierson wrote:

> I have been granted a vision of a magnificent literature enshrining the thoughts of great men from generation to generation through three thousand years. I have been able to stroll through enchanted gardens of poesy beginning with the happy carefree hymns of the Vedas, continuing through great epics, through the magic of Indian drama and the consummate world witchery of Kalidasa... Truth have I gathered from many a tree of knowledge from the ripe Pandit, strong in his monism, acute in thought, crystal clear in his exposition and from the simple peasant chatting in his rude patois under the village tree, steeped in the deepest superstition, yet quick with the living faith in the fatherhood of God... Hidden under religiosity have I found religion, hidden under legend history, wisdom have I found in the proverbs of the unlettered hand...

Amongst the numerous awards Grierson received was an honorary Doctorate of Letters (D. Litt.) from the University of Dublin in June 1902, Order of Merit (OM) in 1928, and the Sir William Jones Gold Medal (established by the Asiatic Society of Bengal) in 1929. He was appointed CIE in 1894 and knighted as a Knight Commander of the Order of the Indian Empire in 1912. He received several other honorary degrees from the universities of Halle, Cambridge and Oxford. He was fellow of the British Academy from 1917 to

1939, and was president of the Gypsy Lore Society in 1927. He was also an honorary member of the Nagari Pracharini Sabha at Varanasi.

After a long illustrious life, Sir George Abraham Grierson passed away at the age of 90 on 9 March 1941. A literary award named as the Dr George Grierson Award was instituted in India in honour of the great linguist. It was to be given by Central Hindi Directorate to outstanding works in Hindi literature as well to experts promoting the Hindi language abroad. The Dr George Grierson Award carries five lakh rupees, a citation and a shawl.

11

JAMES FERGUSSON

The Architectural Historian

'Her (India's) arts are more original and more varied, and her forms of civilization present an ever-changing variety, such as are nowhere else to be found. What, however, really renders India so interesting as an object of study is that it is now a living entity. Greece and Rome are dead and have passed away, and we are living so completely in the midst of modern Europe that we cannot get outside to contemplate it as a whole. But India is a complete cosmos in itself; bounded in the north by the Himalayas, on the south by the sea, on the east by impenetrable jungles, and only on the west having one door of communication open to the other world.'

– James Fergusson in *The History of Indian and Eastern Architecture*, 1876

1840

JAMES FERGUSSON HAD BEEN ON HORSEBACK FOR MANY MONTHS, riding through perilous terrain covered by forests and crisscrossed by deep ravines before reaching the hilly region of Aurangabad in western India. He heard the distant sound of gushing water; that was the sound he had been waiting because a waterfall marked the location of the wondrous cave temples that he had come in search of.

Before embarking on the trip, he did extensive study of the area and also spoke to the local people in an effort to locate the Saptakunda (Seven Ponds), a huge waterfall just behind the Ajanta Caves. He rode on with renewed enthusiasm towards the sound and soon found himself in a clearing on the hill. Looking down, he beheld, for the first time, the ancient rock-cut caves nestling in the forest above the Waghora river.

The caves had been cut into a horseshoe-shaped rock face around the river. He wondered if this was where, about a decade ago, a young lieutenant by the name of James Alexander had accidentally come upon these caves while out on a hunting trip. Fergusson was overwhelmed. He had never seen anything like this.

For many hours, he remained engrossed in studying the caves adorned with paintings and rock-cut sculptures. He guessed that the earliest caves belonged to the second century BCE. But all of them did not belong to the same era. These caves were evidently built over a long period of time. There were 29 of them, 3 of which were *chaityas* (abode of the monks), and the rest were *viharas* (the prayer halls; each containing a stupa or Buddhist shrine). The oldest amongst the caves at Ajanta were the cluster of four caves in the centre. They belonged to the pre-Christian era and formed the nucleus from which the caves radiated outwards.

The most beautiful and interesting of the caves were cave numbers 16 and 17. Fergusson was fascinated by the structure of cave 16, which had 20 pillars, 16 cells and a sanctuary with a seated figure of the Buddha. Every inch of the walls were covered with frescoes representing scenes from Buddhist Jatakas, the legends of the Buddha's life. The ceiling had arabesques and ornaments covering the entire surface.

Fergusson took extensive notes on everything he saw before deciding to capture the majestic grandeur of this ancient Indian architecture on paper. He had brought along an optical instrument called 'camera lucida' – a device for accurate sketching of objects by reflecting an object's image on a sheet of paper lying before the viewer and enabling them to trace it with a pencil. Thus, by fixing one of the adjustable metal arms of the instrument on his drawing board and pressing one eye close to the glass prism attached to the other arm, Fergusson was able to see a reflection of the structure in the prism in front of him and, simultaneously, a refracted image of the scene superimposed on the paper on his drawing board. He then traced the outlines to get a precise sketch.

Despite this interest in ancient architecture and art, Fergusson was neither an artist nor a scholar. At that point of time, he was a successful indigo merchant running his own business in Calcutta. There were no indications in his early life that one day James Fergusson would be hailed as a pioneering archaeologist by none other than Heinrich Schliemann, the German archaeologist and excavator. Fergusson himself admitted in the preface of one of his books, *An Historical Inquiry into the True Principles of Beauty in Art: More Especially with Reference to Architecture*, that he had 'written, and, perhaps also thought, more about the state of the money market, indigo, sugar, silk and such like articles' than he did about architecture, painting or sculpture.

Although he never received any formal training in the subject, through his arduous research and his ability to classify the results according to his own interpretations, Fergusson was able to bring to the attention of the West to the beauty and grandeur of India's architecture.

James Fergusson was born in Ayr, Scotland on 22 January 1808 to Dr William Fergusson, an army surgeon. He was educated at the Royal High School in Edinburgh and later at a private school at Hounslow. He prepared for a career with Fairlie Fergusson & Co., a firm of Calcutta merchants with which the Fergusson family was connected.

According to Professor M.S. Ramaswami Iyengar's chapter on Fergusson in *Eminent Orientalists*, he went to India in 1835 and began working in Calcutta with his elder brother, William, who at the time was a partner with Fairlie Fergusson & Co. However, he was out of job soon, as his brothers company failed. Not long after, Fergusson set up his own business. He bought a share in an indigo factory and became an indigo planter in Bengal.

Indigo cultivation in Bengal dates back to 1777 and it became profitable because of the demand for blue dye in Europe. Blue dye was extracted from indigo plants and was a valuable commodity until about the 1890s, when a commercially viable manufacturing process was invented. By mid-1840s, Fergusson had made sufficient money for the rest of his life and returned to England. But commercial success does not sum up his life; had that been so, Fergusson's name would have been long forgotten.

Fergusson had been attracted to art and architecture from his student days, and that remained his lifelong obsession. Coming to India proved to be a blessing because it was here that his inquisitive mind, innate love for art, and obsession for architecture and design found a fertile soil. It inspired him to get involved in scholarly studies on his own without proper training in architecture.

During his initial years in India, Fergusson became aware of numerous edifices of great antiquity dotting the countryside. These were not primitive prehistoric monuments, but sophisticated structures adorned with elaborate carvings and paintings of high-level workmanship. They had somehow remained uncharted and unknown for centuries. Fergusson thought that there was a vast scope there for studies not undertaken before. As per an article in 'The Popular Science Monthly', he had 'found in India an attractive field, and novel in many of its features, for the cultivation of this taste'. He was excited at prospect of inspecting India's ancient monuments, and embarked on a long tour of the subcontinent.

Between 1835 and 1842, Fergusson went on long tours visiting various locations famous for their architectural remains. Since this was a period before the introduction of railways in India, he travelled mostly by camel, horse, bullock cart and even palki. He journeyed across the country, battling harsh climate and dangerous terrain to arrive at faraway places such as Thanjavur, Chidambaram, Mamallapuram, Ajanta, Ellora, Karle, Mandu, Badoli, Deeg, Ranakpur, Mount

Abu, Delhi, Agra and Lucknow. Throughout his travels, he collected materials for his work on the art and architecture of India.

While earlier orientalists got their information from ancient texts or written information, Fergusson attempted to discover India's past through 'the imperishable records in the rocks, or on sculptures and carvings, which necessarily represented the faith and feelings of those who executed them, and which retain their original impress to this day', as per his words in the *History of Indian and Eastern Architecture.* Besides his own studies and laborious field notes, Fergusson also collected information from the local people and prepared detailed notes of every monument he visited. He added accurate sketches made with the aid of his camera lucida, which he carried everywhere with him.

It was his firm belief that 'no one has a right to say that he understands the history of architecture' who leaves out of view the art and architecture of India. However, practically no in-depth work had been done on the architecture and sculpture of India before Fergusson's efforts.

It's worth keeping in mind that by the time Fergusson arrived in the country, India was no longer the land of mystery that it had been in the past. Certain aspects about the country's past had already been revealed; for instance, the Gandhara art of the northwest had been discovered and the Brahmi script had been deciphered. Also, India had come to the notice of the Western world through landscape artists such as William Hodges, and Thomas and William Daniell.

Although those beautifully illustrated publications had an impact in popularizing oriental architecture, the works of Hodges had glaring inaccuracies, while the Daniells' drawings, according to Fergusson, were highly romanticized and often far removed from reality. Mildred Archer and R.W. Lightbown mention, in their 1982 book *India Observed*, that Fergusson felt that the work of the earlier artists, though extremely valuable as art, 'entirely destroys its value as one of information and instruction'.

Another book of the time that threw some light on the architectural heritage of ancient India was *The Essays on the Architecture of the Hindus* by Ram Raz, an English master in the college of St. George who would later become a magistrate in Mysore state. This book was published posthumously in 1834 by the Royal Asiatic Society. However, it was a translation of *Hindu Shilpa Shastra* – an architectural dissertation originally written in Sanskrit – and not an original study of ancient Hindu monuments.

It was Fergusson's firm belief that old buildings tell us more about people, their culture, their hopes and desires, more than poetry or literature. In the preface of the first volume of his *History of Architecture in All Countries*, he wrote,

> ...men who had a hankering after immortality were forced to build their aspirations into the walls of their tombs or of their temples. Those who had poetry in their souls, in nine cases out of ten expressed it by the more familiar vehicle of sculpture or painting rather than in writing. To me it appears that to neglect these in trying to understand the manners and customs or the history of an ancient people, is to throw away one half, and generally the most valuable half, in some cases the whole, of the evidence bearing on the subject.

He lamented in the *History of Indian and Eastern Architecture* that 'though every problem of anthropology or ethnography can be studied in India more easily than anywhere else... (yet) India and Indian matters fail to interest because to most Europeans they are new and unfamiliar.' Although an avowed admirer of classical Greece and Rome, Fergusson's fascination for Indian art stemmed from his belief that 'Architecture in India is still a living art, practised on the principles which caused its wonderful development in Europe in the 12th and 13th centuries.... In India and in India alone the student of architecture has a chance of seeing the real principle of the art in action.'

Fergusson was extremely critical of the type of architecture that was in vogue in contemporary Europe. Instead, he praises Indian masons in his *History of Indian and Eastern Architecture*: 'The Indian builders *think* only of what they are doing and how they can best produce the effect they desire.' He says that in the European system, it is considered more essential that a building, especially in structural detail, should be a correct copy of something else, than good in itself or appropriate to its purpose; hence the difference in the result.

Fergusson also felt that the mode in which the art has been practiced in India was clear and intelligible. Elaborating on the subject, he writes,

> [C]ertain qualities the Indian buildings are unrivalled. They display an exuberance of fancy, a lavishness of labour, and an elaboration of detail to be found nowhere else. ...the Indian buildings stand alone. They consequently fill up a great gap in the knowledge of our subject, which without them would remain a void.

In a letter to his sister, quoted by Peter Kohane, he dwells on his capacity to appreciate the beauty of buildings that eluded other Westerners. And expresses his sense of wonderment on his visit to the Palace of Shah Jahan at Agra. He writes, 'I wandered from one court to another, ...bewildered by the beauty that was around me on every side, and lost in amazement that such works of art that I have never seen equalled should be so little known or esteemed.'

Fergusson believed that because India comprised different ethnic groups, each ethnic group retained its old beliefs and feelings, and these were reflected in their art. Thus, Fergusson's classification was based on categories, rather than the regions they belonged to. Accordingly, Hindu architecture could be classified into three styles: the Indo-Aryan or northern style, the Dravidian style, and the Chalukyan style.

The Indo-Aryan Style, also referred to as the northern style by Fergusson, existed in the regions north of the Tapti and Mahanadi rivers and included some of the beautiful temples of Bhubaneswar that were built after 950 CE, developing the same way as Muslim architecture developed in Delhi. This style is also in evidence at Khajuraho, Gwalior, Udaipur and Deeg. In his own words in the *History of Indian and Eastern Architecture*, Fergusson felt that the Khajuraho temples 'are the most beautiful in form as well as the most elegant in detail of any of the temples now standing in India.'

However, it may be a misnomer to call it 'northern style' as the style cannot be described in its ethnographical and geographical relation. Ironically, Fergusson mentions that there are perhaps more temples in Orissa and, if we admit, 'the Jains who adopted this style, they are ten times more frequent in Gujarat, Rajasthan and the valley of the Nerbudda (Narmada) than in the valley of the Ganges'.

According to him, identifying the Dravidian style is simpler as it is limited to people speaking Tamil, Telugu or some cognate dialect. The Dravidian style extends as far north as the mouth of the Krishna river, including the present-day Andhra Pradesh and Telangana. A Dravidian temple can be identified by the *Vimana*, the structure over the inner sanctum in the Hindu temples of South India and Odisha in East India. The *vimana* is the tallest structure of the temple and is typically structured like a stepped pyramid with several stories. It invariably has (a) The porches or *mandapas*; (b) *Gopurams,* the main features in the gateways around the temples; and (c) pillared halls or *choultries*.

According to Fergusson in *History of Indian and Architecture*, the temples at Pattadakal are very pure examples of the Dravidian style of architecture; Rathas of Mamallapuram are embryos of the Dravidian style and of the Kailasa temple Ellora, absolutely unique in the whole of India. The temples of Chidambaram are the oldest and are located in southern India and portions of them are gems of Dravidian art.

The Chalukyan style, on the other hand, is a mixture of the northern and southern styles, combining elegance of outline with elaboration of detail in animal friezes. Its distinctive traits include a polygonal or star-shaped plan instead of a square; a high, curved plinth, following the outline of the temple; and a low pyramidal roof in horizontal layers instead of the high *sikhara,* or spire, with vertical lines. Examples of this style are the temples at Somnathpur and Halebid built by Hoysala Ballalas in the period from the eleventh to the thirteenth century CE. A characteristic feature of the Chalukyan design is that the temples stand on a terrace 3 feet high and 10 to 15 feet wide.

About the Halebid temple, Fergusson noted in the *History of Indian and Eastern Architecture* that some of the pillars in the inner part of the temple are of black hornblende and have a dazzling polish. He further states, 'some of these (friezes) are carved with a minute elaboration of detail which can only be reproduced by photography, and may probably be considered as one of the most marvellous exhibitions of human labour to be found even in the patient East.' Fergusson places the Halebid temple and the Parthenon as the two extremes of architectural art and says,

> ...there would be few things more interesting or more instructive than to institute a comparison between [the Halebid temple] and the Parthenon at Athens...they form the two opposite poles, the alpha and omega of architectural design; but they are the best examples of their class, and between these two extremes lies the whole range of the art.

According to his *History of Architecture in All Countries*, every part of the Halebid temple 'exhibits a joyous exuberance of fancy scorning every mechanical restraint. All that is wild in human faith or warm in human feeling is found portrayed on these walls'.

Fergusson also found that Indo-Islamic architecture (also known as the Indo-Saracenic architecture) had 13 different styles. They varied in the regions north and south of the river Narmada, as per his book the *History of Indian and Eastern Architecture*.

North of the River styles: The Ghazni style though not originally from India, had the most significant influence on the Indian styles. It was the means by which the architecture of the Islamic world was introduced into India.

The Pathan style, however, represented a blending of Hindu and Islamic styles. Since the Pathans were invaders, they had not brought with them masons, artists or architects from their land; but they found among their new subjects talented workers capable of carrying out any design propounded by them. The local masons and sculpturers were naturally guided by the traditions then prevailing in India. Despite of the difference between the Indian and the Islamic styles, there were two points of resemblance that favoured their fusion.

One characteristic feature of many Hindu temples as well as mosques was the open court, encompassed by chambers or colonnades, and such temples naturally lent themselves to conversion into mosques and would be the first to be adapted for that purpose by the conquerors. Another fundamental characteristic that linked the two styles was the inherently decorative and ornamental style of both Islamic and Hindu art.

The best specimens of the Pathan style is the Quwwat-ul Islam Mosque (earlier known as Qubbat-ul-Islam) which stands next to the Qutab Minar. It is the most beautiful example of its type known to exist anywhere. The tomb of Iltutmish is another instance of Hindu art applied to Mohammedan purposes and is the oldest tomb known to exist in India. Also, the tomb of Sher Shah in Sasaram is a fine example of the late Pathan style.

The Varied Individual styles: When the central authority became weak after the death of Ala-ud-din, outlying provinces declared themselves independent and exhibited their individuality by inventing a style according to personal taste of the ruler. The first of these was the Jaunpur style adopted by the brilliant but short-lived Sharqi dynasty (1394-1476 CE) of Jaunpur in present-day Uttar Pradesh. They adorned their capital and other cities with a series of magnificent buildings showing marked influence of Hindu art. Atala Devi Masjid (completed 1408 CE) is a brilliant specimen of the Jaunpur style. The style adopted by the rulers of Gujarat (1396-1572 CE) was richer and more varied than that of Jaunpur. They too borrowed a great deal from the architecture of the Hindus and Jains among whom they were located. Malwa style existed while Malwa was an independent state (1401-1569 CE) and adorned the palaces and mosques at their capital, Mandu. Gaur and Malda style was prevalent when Bengal was a separate kingdom (1203-1573 CE). During this period, the capitals were adorned with many splendid edifices. It was a mixed type of architecture characterized by the use of bricks in the main buildings, with subsidiary buildings made of stone. The Adina Masjid at Pandua is a fine example of this style. It was built in 1368 CE and is renowned for its beauty.

Besides, the above mentioned Indo-Islamic styles north of the river Narmada, he classified the South of the River Narmada style, which could be further classified into three other well marked styles the Bahmani style, Bijapur style and Southern style. The Bahmani style belonged to the Bahmani dynasty that ruled first at Gulbarga from 1347 CE and later at Bidar from 1426 CE. The celebrated Bijapur style was marked by a grandeur of conception and boldness in construction unequalled by any edifices erected in India. The Southern style is that of the Qutb Shahi dynasty of Golconda (1512-1672 CE).

One by one all these dynasties were absorbed into the great Mughal empire (1526-1750 CE) founded by Babar. Fergusson also identified a style of Muslim art prevailing in Sind, the architecture in Avadh that he designated as the bastard style, and the style adopted by the short-lived dynasty (1700-1799 CE) at Mysore.

Fergusson was the pioneer of archaeological scholarship in India whose contribution to the study and classification of Indian architecture was immense. Even his harsh critic E.B. Havell had to rely on Fergusson's research for chronological facts and measurements of buildings while writing a book on Indian architecture in 1913.

As an art historian, Fergusson deserved better than the misrepresentation of him by Partha Mitter, an emeritus professor of art history at the University of Sussex, in his book *Much Maligned Monsters.* The fact that Fergusson was far ahead of his time in the appreciation of Indian art was acknowledged even by Havell.

A leading light of conservation, Fergusson was one of the earliest people to appreciate the urgent need to preserve and restore the ancient monuments in India. He did this much before the Ancient Monuments Bill was passed in 1904. It hurt him to see innumerable monuments of great antiquity lying neglected and uncared for throughout the country.

Fergusson was very critical of the colonial government's failure to restore the priceless heritage buildings of India; specially in the case of one of the earliest temples known to exist at Halebid, a small detached shrine dedicated to Lord Shiva known as Kedaresvara. It was covered with the very best of Indian art, arranged to not interfere with the outlines of the building but still impart to it an astonishing richness. Fergusson wrote in his 1876 book *History of Indian and Eastern Architecture*,

> In a very few years this building will be entirely destroyed by the trees, which have fastened their roots in the joints of the stone. A few years more, if some steps are not taken to save it, it will have perished entirely, a very small sum would save it; and as the country is in our charge, it is hoped that the expenditure will not be grudged.

But no attention was paid to this warning and Fergusson's gloomy predictions came true.

About certain other buildings in Delhi and Ajmer, Fergusson wrote, 'They deserve the protecting care of the government. These have been shamefully neglected and most barbarously ill-treated.' However, India had to wait till Lord Curzon arrived to personally supervise the restoration and preservation of ancient monuments. Curzon also appointed a director-general for archaeology in India.

Among Fergusson's books, the most remarkable is *History of Architecture*. Beginning as a handbook in 1855, it was expanded to four volumes in 1875. The first two volumes were titled *A History of Ancient and Medieval Architecture* and the fourth, *A History of the Modern Style of Architecture*. It is the third volume that was about India: *A History of Indian and Eastern Architecture.* It was initially published in 1876 as a 700-page tome with 400 illustrations, most of them devoted to India. A second edition was published in 1910, revised and edited by J. Burgess.

Fergusson left India in 1845 and settled down at his house in London. He spent the rest of his life studying building designs. He held many positions in England, including Inspector of Public Buildings and Monuments, and received the gold medal for architecture from the Institute of British Architects.

However, the greatest achievement of this pioneering archaeologist and architectural historian is the systematizing of the history of Indian architecture. Heinrich Schliemann dedicated his great work on Tiryns to Fergusson, praising him as 'The historian of architecture, eminent alike for his knowledge of art and the original genius that he has applied to the solution of some of its most difficult problems', as quoted in the *Dictionary of Indian Biography* from 1889.

James Fergusson breathed his last in London on 9 January 1886. Robert Elwall writes in his essay on Fergusson in the 'RSA Journal':

> Fergusson put architectural history on a more professional footing, freeing it from a dry rendition of dates and facts. He not only considerably widened its scope but, by the way in which he dispensed with myth and marshalled his sources, he also introduced a new rigour and discipline. He further broke new grounds by his use of photographs, by his thought-provoking comparisons of buildings far distant

in time and place, and by the way in which he attempted to establish linkages with the society that produced them. These were Fergusson's legacies.

12

BRIAN HOUGHTON HODGSON

The Founder of the True Study of Buddhism

'Brian Hodgson died in 1894, in his ninety-fifth year. Had he died seventy years previously, he would have been mourned as the most brilliant young scholar whom the Indian Civil Service has produced. Had he died in middle life, he would have been remembered as the masterly diplomatist who held quiet the kingdom of Nepal and the warlike Himalayan races throughout the disasters of the Afghan War. Had he died at three-score years of age, he would have been honoured as the munificent Englishman who enriched the museums of Europe with his collections, enlarged the old boundaries of more than one science, and opened up a new field of original research.'

– Sir William Wilson Hunter in *Life of Brian Houghton Hodgson*, 1896[1]

[1] Sir William Wilson Hunter was a Scottish historian, statistician, a compiler and a member of the Indian Civil Service.

1819

AN ENGLISH OFFICER, BARELY 20 YEARS OLD, HAD BEEN TRAVELLING in a *palki* (palanquin) for almost a month now. He was on his way from the warm Gangetic plains to the mountainous region of Kumaon, situated on the outer range of the spurs of the Himalayas. The young man looked totally drained out. He had been on the road for almost a month, but the journey was far from over.

A sudden commotion made him look up. He saw, right in front of him, a thick dense forest standing like a wall blocking further progress. The only way to continue the journey was by riding on elephants, which were arranged quickly. He continued past waterless springs and dry riverbeds to a point from where he suddenly saw snow-capped mountains ahead of him. The awe-inspiring mountains combined with the sublime beauty of the terrain took his breath away. This was the territory where he would be spending the early years of his service in India as assistant commissioner of Kumaon.

This young Englishman was Brian Houghton Hodgson, an East India Company employee. He was on his way to take charge of his position. Could he, at that moment, have guessed that within the next few years he would become famous? And not for his official position, but as the discoverer of the literature of northern Buddhism as preserved in both Sanskrit and Tibetan manuscripts?

Brian Houghton Hodgson was born at Prestbury, Cheshire to Brian and Catherine. Interestingly, his father, grandfather as well as great-grandfather were all named Brian. There is uncertainty about the year of his birth but we can assume it was 1800. He was the second of seven children.

The senior Hodgson was a banker, but became bankrupt because of some bad investments, and the family had to go through a great deal of financial difficulties. However, with the help of relatives and friends, Brian's education did not suffer. They moved to Macclesfield, a county of Cheshire in England, and Brian was admitted to Macclesfield Grammar School before being selected for a writership in the Bengal Civil Service in February 1816.

He then began his training at the East India Company's college in Haileybury. While waiting to take the entrance exam, Hodgson was placed as a guest in the house of Thomas Robert Malthus, a famous English economist and demographer who was the professor of history and political economy at Haileybury at that time. His mentorship and personal kindness during that time proved extremely beneficial for Hodgson.

Students at Haileybury were encouraged to take up local languages. Hodgson had a great aptitude for languages, and ranked at the top of his class in Bengali, Persian and Hindi. As a result, he was allowed to choose the presidency to which he would be posted. Hodgson chose the Bengal Presidency, and arrived in Calcutta in 1818.

At first, Hodgson continued his studies in Indian law and languages for a year at Fort William. However, he fell ill with a liver condition and was advised to transfer to a hill station. As a result, he was posted to the cooler climes of Kumaon, situated in the foothills of the western Himalayas.

From 1819, he held the post of assistant commissioner in the Kumaon region under George William Traill, who was the commissioner. After working for a year in Kumaon, he was promoted and appointed as assistant resident in Nepal, working under Edward Gardner, the first British Resident of the court of Nepal. This was the period when he became interested in researching Buddhism and began collecting Sanskrit manuscripts.

Hodgson was recalled to Calcutta in 1822 to act as deputy secretary in the Persian department of the Foreign Office. It was an important position, but he could not continue because of another breakdown in his health. He returned to Kathmandu in 1824, working as a postmaster. Hodgson became a Resident in January 1833 but throughout his stay there, he suffered from ill health. To ease his condition, he gave up meat and alcohol in 1837.

Because of his poor health, he was soon condemned to isolation. However, Hodgson turned his solitude into a unique opportunity by devoting all his free time to original research. Between 1829 and 1843, Hodgson extended the scope of his research to cover not only Buddhism but also zoology, and ethnography. He produced a number of papers on the languages, literature and religion of the Nepalese people. He also collected manuscripts in Bengali, Persian and Sanskrit, which he sent to institutions in Europe and India. However, Hodgson's most prized possession were the 80 Buddhist manuscripts which he had acquired in Nepal.

In 1833, Hodgson became the Resident in Nepal. It was a tumultuous period in Nepal politics. And Hodgson played a crucial role in keeping Nepal peaceful during the First Afghan War, in the course of which the British army was annihilated. This was an extremely perilous situation for the British, and it could have been worse for them if Nepal had tried to take advantage of it. However, Hodgson's tact and diplomacy enabled him to steer through the troubled waters. His brilliant success in the operation was achieved partly because of his friendly relationship with the Nepal chiefs and partly due to the extraordinary reputation he had acquired amongst the locals for his life of austerity, which had earned him the sobriquet 'the Hermit of the Himalayas'.

However, even though Hodgson had succeeded in the difficult task, he was suddenly dismissed from the residency of Nepal on the grounds of defiance of the Governor General's orders. Henry Lawrence was sent as his replacement in Nepal, while Hodgson was transferred to the lowly post of assistant sub-commissioner at Shimla. Hodgson resigned forthwith. Even though, subsequently, Ellenborough decided to reinstate him it had become a matter of pride for Hodgson and he set sail for England, retiring from service in 1843 at the age of 43.

During his stay in Nepal, Hodgson had studied Buddhist literature and religion deeply, and concluded that the literature of northern Buddhism was distinct from Pali, or southern Buddhism. The division of Buddhism based on the Pali scriptures preserved in Sri Lanka was called southern Buddhism, and the division of Buddhism mainly based on the Sanskrit scriptures transmitted from India to Central Asia and China was referred to as northern Buddhism.

Hodgson spent a considerable sum of money on the purchasing and copying of Buddhist or Sanskrit manuscripts. He employed a local staff of copyists and draughtsmen to copy Buddhist manuscripts. He was focused on devising ways and means of procuring accurate information associated with Buddhism. It was not easy as initially he was met with resistance from the locals, who were not inclined to share their sacred texts with a foreigner.

The breakthrough came when he obtained a list of Buddhist sacred texts hidden away in the monasteries of Nepal with the aid of a venerable pandit. Having won the pandit's confidence, Hodgson persuaded him to gradually procure copies of the most important of the manuscripts. He then drew up a series of questions on the religion and philosophy of Buddhism as it existed in Nepal. Hodgson's unwearied search for Sanskrit manuscripts and his transcription of Hindu texts eventually endeared him to the local pandits.

From the time of Hodgson's return to Nepal in 1824, a stream of manuscripts, specimens and antiquarian curios began to flow into the Asiatic Society of Bengal. Hodgson was an avid compiler of ancient manuscripts. He collected Tibetan manuscripts and texts mainly from the archives of the Buddhist monastery of Swayambhunath, and also from the monks who came on pilgrimage to Nepal annually. In this unexplored field, Hodgson found treasure troves everywhere. His only regret was that his resources were limited. As quoted by William Wilson Hunter in his 1896 book *Life of Brian Houghton*, 'Nepal has many old valuables going fast to oblivion, and Tibet probably has many more. But these things are very expensive. What I have already sent cost me sundry rupees numerous to be mentioned yet given most cheerfully.'

These manuscripts had survived due to a number of reasons. Mainly, it was due to the dry climate of Nepal, which was suited for the preservation of documents. Another reason was their isolated location, which had saved them from the havoc of the Muslim invasion that had resulted in the annihilation of a great many literary treasures of India. Also, while brittle palm leaves were being used for manuscripts in India during that period, early use of paper in Tibet and Nepal resulted in better preservation of manuscripts even in the eleventh century. Thus, Buddhist *sutras* and *tantras* long lost in India were preserved in Nepal.

According to Hunter, Hodgson had 'collected a larger body of original documents on Buddhism than had up to that time been ever gathered either in Asia or in Europe'. The oldest manuscripts sent by Hodgson to England belonged to the twelfth century. These manuscripts were of great benefit to scholars and helped them in their investigation and research. It is not an exaggeration to say that almost all the original work among northern Buddhist manuscripts in France, Great Britain and India during the latter half of the nineteenth century had been based upon materials collected by Hodgson. Dr Rajendra Lal Mitra's monumental work *The Sanskrit Buddhist Literature of Nepal* is primarily based on the material supplied by Hodgson to the Asiatic Society of Bengal.

Hodgson sent about 147 of these manuscripts to Société Asiatique. Hunter notes that these caught the attention of the French oriental scholar Eugene Burnouf, regarded by many as the founding father of modern Buddhist scientific studies, who refers to Hodgson as '*fondateur de la véritable étude du Buddhisme par les textes et les monuments*', or the 'founder of the true study of Buddhism through texts and monuments'.

Burnouf's great work on the history of Buddhism, *Introduction à l'histoire du Bouddhisme indien* that was published in Paris in 1876, was based on the manuscripts presented by Hodgson. France honoured Hodgson with the Legion of Honour, Institut de France appointed him a corresponding member and Société Asiatique commemorated Hodgson's service with a gold medal.

Hodgson rendered an equally important service to European scholarship with his collection of Tibetan classics. These classics are embodied in two vast encyclopaedias of sacred learning and philosophy. In 1845, Hodgson endowed the British Museum with the Tibetan translation of the *Prajna-paramita*, a vast work in five volumes and 1,00,000 verses. Hodgson sent four times the number of manuscripts in Tibetan to the Asiatic Society of Bengal.

He himself wrote extensively on Buddhism and other related matters. His first articles on Buddhism appeared in *Asiatic Researches* and 'Transactions of the Royal Asiatic Society'. In 1841, he published *Illustration of the Literature and Religion of the Buddhists*. He also wrote *Essays on the Languages, Literature, and Religion of Nepal and Tibet*. Burnouf hailed Hodgson's contribution to *Asiatic Researches* as 'full of entirely new ideas on the languages, literature and religion of the Buddhists of Nepal and Tibet.'

There had been large collections of Sanskrit manuscripts in the monasteries of Nepal, the existence of which had never been suspected known until Hodgson discovered them. Scholars have expressed their astonishment and general admiration at the perfect lucidity with which Hodgson not only unravelled but also elucidated coherently the extremely complicated concept of the four philosophic systems of Nepalese Buddhists.

Hodgson's illustrations of the literature and origin of the Buddhists impacted a whole generation of European writing according to Hunter, including specialists like Sir Alexander Cunningham, who wrote to Hodgson, 'I found in your work the only clear and intelligible account of Buddhism.'

After retiring from service, Hodgson went back to England in 1843, but returned to India in 1845 as a private citizen in order to complete the research he had been working on. However, he was not given permission to return to Nepal as he was no longer on official duty. Undaunted, he decided to settle in Darjeeling, which was similar to Nepalese climate and conditions.

Besides delving into Buddhism, Hodgson also investigated the hill races, devoting himself to the study of non-Aryan races of India. He believed that the racial affinities could be identified on the basis of linguistics. Hodgson's ethnographic studies of the aborigines of India began with his observation of three tribes of the sub-Himalayan areas. He wrote essays on the Kocch, Bodo and Dhimal tribes and had them published in Calcutta in 1847.

It was a pioneering work on the subject and brought out in bold and simple terms the difference between the non-Aryan races and the Aryan dwellers in the plains. His work was widely hailed. Hunter mentions that the leading British ethnologist Robert Gordon Latham acknowledged it to be 'a model of ethnological monograph', and a scholar and diplomat by the name of Moris Bunsen described it as 'our highest living authority and best informant of the ethnology of the native races of India.'

In 1849, Hodgson wrote on the physical geography of the Himalayas after studying the flowing patterns of two great rivers, the Brahmaputra and the Tsang Po. At the time, the Brahmaputra had a stretch of 800 miles along the Tibetan trough that was yet to be explored. It was only known that a great river called the Tsang Po flowed eastwards along the Central Asian trough, while another great river called the Brahmaputra surged through the eastern Himalayas into Assam.

Although there were some theories that these two rivers formed different sections of the same stream, these were still only conjectures at the time. It was Hodgson's inferences while in Nepal and the geographical details which he supplied, that proved these deductions. In 1839, as per Hunter, the East India Company's special envoy to Bhutan wrote that the evidences of the Tsang Po and the Brahmaputra being one and the same river was 'greatly strengthened by Mr Hodgson's manuscript map forwarded to the Surveyor-General.'

Hodgson was also the first person to identify tea as the most suitable of the subtropical crops to grow in the Himalayas. Although the experimental plantation of tea had already been ongoing in Assam since 1834, not much thought had been given to growing tea in the Himalayan districts. Hodgson successfully experimented in growing tea in Nepal. Tea seeds and plants procured from China through Kashmiri merchants were sown in the residency garden at Kathmandu. They had flourished in abundance, convincing Hodgson that Darjeeling, with its close resemblance to Nepal both in climate and topography, was ideally suited to the plantation of tea. Tea-plantation has since had a success in Darjeeling that not even Hodgson could anticipate.

Hodgson also made some significant contributions as a zoologist. Starting from 1824, he began to study characteristics of the Himalayan animals. He identified the wild dog of Tibet, the shawl goat, the four-horned sheep and the yak. He published a much-acclaimed paper on Himalayan mammals in 1826. Hodgson also discovered the chiru, a new specimen of Tibetan antelope. He sent a specimen to Dr Clarke Abel, the natural scientist who described it and named it *Pantholops Hodgsoni*, after Hodgson.

Hodgson gave the scientific name of *Porcula salvania* (*salvania* being a combination of sal + *van,* the Sanskrit word for forest) to a species of pygmy hog inhabiting the sal forest of the region. Hodgson contributed 51 papers on the Himalayan mammals to the Asiatic Society of Bengal, and a further 29 papers to scientific journals.

He pursued this interest till 1858, the year he left India. Charles Darwin, while discussing the origin of the domestic dog in his *Variation of Animals and Plants under Domestication*, mentions that Hodgson succeeded in taming the dhole, an Indian wild dog, and found that they were as intelligent as regular dogs.

Ornithology was also a big part of Hodgson's interest in the natural sciences. Even though his research in ornithology was limited to Nepal and Sikkim, he also gained a lot of knowledge of birds of India. According to A.O. Hume, a noted ornithologist who was also the founder of the Indian National Congress, Hodgson identified 150 new species of birds.

The papers Hodgson submitted to the Asiatic Society of Bengal and other scientific journals were subsequently used by many eminent writers. Hume himself quoted extensively from the Hodgson's notes in his two seminal books, *Game Birds of India* and *Nests and Eggs of Indian Birds*, and said that Hodgson's name will be 'remembered, cherished, and revered' by future ornithologists.

Scientifically accurate drawings and sketches of Indian birds and Himalayan mammals were created by local artists under Hodgson's supervision. These visuals supplemented his writings and added value to Hodgson's work. Hodgson also discovered 39 species of mammals and 124 species of birds which had not been written about earlier. His zoological collections, which he presented to the British Museum (in 1843 and 1858), contained 10,499 specimens, besides his collection of a huge number of drawings and coloured sketches of Indian animals, produced by three native artists who had been working under his supervision.

Hunter writes that the images of birds depicted included new species as well as 'several hundred other already recorded ones, and in many cases their nests and eggs also. ...And above all, the invaluable notes as to food, ...eggs, station, habits constituting as a whole materials for a life-history of many hundred species such as... no ornithologist had ever previously garnered.'

Hodgson's work on birds can be considered his prime achievement in zoology. He had gathered 9,512 specimens which represented 672 bird species. He is responsible for describing of 80 bird species for the first time, while the rest of the credits are given to others who used Hodgson's specimens to describe species.

Apart from his interests in the natural world, Hodgson was also involved in debates of culture and language. During the first twenty years of his service, a controversy had been raging on whether the language for higher education in India should be English or the classical languages of India. The dispute reached its zenith in 1835 when Lord Macaulay was a member of the Supreme Council of India. And, according to Sir George Otto Trevelyan, son of Sir Charles Trevelyan and nephew of Lord Macaulay quoted in the *Life of Brian Houghton Hodgson*, 'All educational action had come to a standstill for some time back, on account of an irreconcilable difference of opinion in the Committee of Public Instruction'.

Hodgson entered the debate at this stage. He was a great supporter of the suitability of vernacular education in India, and vigorously opposed Macaulay's drive for the use of English as a medium of instruction. He endeared himself to Indians by being a champion of popular education in their mother tongues. He wrote a series of essays, for the journal of the Serampore Mission called 'The Friend of India', opining that if education of the Indian public was to become a reality, it must be conducted neither in English nor in classical languages of India but in the living vernacular of each province. In Hodgson's words, quoted by Hunter:

> Taking Bengali as an example, "the language of thirty-seven millions," he pointed out that it had already good dictionaries and grammars, and possessed an adequate "precision and compass", while its close relationship to Sanskrit afforded "means of enrichment by new terms

competent to express any imaginable modification of thought."

He also proposed the establishment of a normal vernacular college for local schoolmasters.

However, Macaulay's arguments influenced the government to choose English as the medium for education. Hodgson dubbed the decision as 'hasty and unfounded.' Though the beginnings of English education can be traced to Macaulay's stance in 1835, the evolution of a comprehensive and coordinated system of education took another twenty years, until the new revision of the East India Company's charter.

The battle which Hodgson had waged finally showed an effect in the new scheme of education outlined for all of India. While recognizing the importance of English instruction, it declared vernacular education to be the basis of state education in India. According to the despatch, recorded by Arthur Howell in the book *Education in British India* published in 1872, 'any acquaintance with improved European knowledge which is to be communicated to a great mass of people can only be conveyed to them through one or other of these vernacular languages.'

Hodgson had a naturally ascetic character. In 1839, he had written to his sister Fanny that he did not eat meat nor drink wine, and preferred Indian food habits. He also led an extremely solitary life. The unstable situation in Nepal those days meant that English civilians could not have any form of social life. Moreover, English women were not allowed to reside in Nepal as it was considered a dangerous outpost.

The extent of Hodgson's isolation can be gauged by one of his letters to Fanny, quoted by Hunter, in which he says, 'My society is unchanging and limited to my suite—a secretary, commander of escort, and surgeon...' The only sports he could indulge in were the ones in which no companion was needed, such as billiards and horse riding; even simple social amusements like a game of cards were not possible. Thus, he resorted to reading, delving into researches about 'the origin, genius, and attainments of various singular races of men inhabiting Nepal.'

Hodgson's lonely situation in Nepal was mitigated to a great extent in 1830 after he married a Muslim lady by the name of Mehrunnisha, with whom he had been in a long-term relationship. Though the marriage may not have had legal sanction, they lived happily as husband and wife until her death. He had two children with her: Henry and Sarah.

According to Hunter's memoir, Hodgson was quite open about the relationship and communicated the news of his marriage to his family back in England. He wrote to his father, 'My boy and girl are well and growing up fast.' To Fanny, he wrote, 'My children are well and their sweet prattle and infant arts soften my heart and amuse my leisure. I shall take them home with me, for I have no idea of putting off the highest duties of our nature at the suggestion of mere vanity or convenience.' Unfortunately, both his children died young, and Mehrunnisha too passed away in 1843.

In 1853, while on a short holiday in England and Holland, Hodgson met Anne Scott, daughter of General Henry Alexander Scott. They got married at the British Embassy at the Hague and a few weeks later he returned to Darjeeling with his wife, where he spent four of the happiest years of his life. However, Anne developed an intolerance of the Darjeeling climate. Also, Hodgson needed to be close to his 92-year-old father, who pined for his companionship. These factors compelled Hodgson to quit India for good in 1858.

Unfortunately, his father passed away before he could reach England. After his return, Hodgson handed over all his papers and manuscripts to the India Office library. Anne died in January 1868, and a year later he married Susan. He had no children with either Anne or Susan.

Brian Hodgson passed away at the age of 94 at his home on Dover Street, London, on 23 May 1894. To really appreciate his legacy, we need to focus upon his work as a collector rather than as an author. Hodgson was the largest and the most munificent collector of ancient texts and vernacular tracts. He spent years in relentless pursuit of ancient manuscripts, and if he could not acquire the original, he would obtain copies and gift them to various libraries. These served as important research matter not just for his contemporaries but also future generations of researchers and scholars.

In 1877, Hodgson was elected a fellow of the Royal Society and, at age of 89, Oxford conferred upon him an honorary degree of Doctor of Civil Law (DCL). However, it is difficult to believe that a man who had been honoured by the membership of almost every learned and scientific body in the West received no recognition or distinction from his own government, despite serving faithfully for so many years.

The *Spectator*, a weekly British magazine, paid Hodgson a tribute by referring to him as 'the noblest Englishman of our century, one of the noblest and rarest men in any country and any period, the type of man richly endowed with energy and capacity who is yet above all mere vulgar ambition, and whose ideals are dissociated from all selfish impulse'.

13

SIR ALEXANDER CUNNINGHAM

The Father of Indian Archaeology

'It is impossible to pass through… any part of the British territories in India without being struck by the neglect with which the greater portion of the architectural remains, and of the traces of by-gone civilization have been treated, though many of these are full of beauty and interest. By "neglect" I do not mean only the omission to restore them, or even to arrest their decay…so far as the Government is concerned, there has been neglect…of investigating and placing on record, for the instruction of future generations, many particulars that might still be rescued from oblivion, and throw light upon the early history of (India)…'

– Alexander Cunningham in Volume one of *Four Reports*, 1871

1871, Calcutta

ALEXANDER CUNNINGHAM HAD JUST COMPLETED WRITING A letter to his friend, and erstwhile Archaeological Assistant, Joseph David Beglar (who was at the time working with the Public Works Department of the Bengal Government), inviting to join him at his office. This was soon after he had accepted Lord Mayo's offer of taking up the post of Director General of the newly established Archaeological Survey of India. From a Second Lieutenant in the army to Director General of Archaeological Survey of India had been an incredible journey.

Born on 23 January 1814 in London, Alexander Cunningham was the second of three sons born to the Scottish poet Alan Cunningham and his wife, Jean Walker. Alexander received his early education at Christ's Hospital, a boarding school in London. His father was a close friend of Sir Walter Scott, and it was through the latter's influence that Alexander and his brother Joseph were given Indian cadetships. They joined the military academy at Addiscombe in 1829 and trained at the Royal Engineers Estate at Chatham.

Cunningham joined the Bengal Engineers and arrived in India on 9 June 1833 as a second lieutenant. He was just 19. He met James Prinsep soon after his arrival in Calcutta. At the time, Prinsep was the assay master of the Calcutta Mint and also secretary to the Asiatic Society of Bengal. He had already made momentous contributions in the field of Indian archaeology. Under Prinsep's tutelage Cunningham began delving into ancient history, geography and numismatics.

Initially, Cunningham served in various executive posts, beginning as ADC or an aide-de-camp to Lord Auckland, the governor-general of India. An ADC works as a personal assistant or secretary to a person of high rank, usually a senior military, police or government officer. During this time, he continued to explore the subcontinent's archaeological sites and relics. After Prinsep's death in 1840, his mantle fell upon his young friend and disciple, Cunningham. Though his stewardship of the Archaeological Survey was still 21 years away, Cunningham had begun to pursue this interest early on in his career.

On 30 March 1840, Cunningham married Alicia Maria Whish. In 1843, he distinguished himself at the battle of Punniar, in which the British forces defeated the Marathas in Gwalior. For the next two years, he was given the difficult responsibility of boundary demarcation with Tibet. When the second Sikh war broke out, he was appointed as a field engineer with the Punjab army and participated in battles at Chillianwalla and Gujrat (Gujarat). Cunningham was honourably mentioned in dispatches and won a number of distinctions.

Cunningham's days as active soldier ended in 1856 when he was made head of administrative work and appointed as chief engineer in the freshly annexed province of Burma (now Myanmar). He was put in charge of organizing a public works department, which he achieved within two years. His next assignment was as a chief engineer of the North-Western Provinces, a region still reeling from the administrative chaos resulting from the Mutiny of 1857.

Despite being very busy with his work, Cunningham had not forgotten his primary passion. Even during his military assignments, he had begun making detailed notes of all the historical sites situated in and around the places wherever he was posted. For instance, during his time in Tibet in 1846, Cunningham made a thorough documentation of all the ruined monuments and sites of the areas of Kashmir, Ladakh and Tibet. His observations and expertise were recorded in great detail in a monograph titled *Temples of Kashmir* and *Ladakh: Physical, Statistical and Historical.*

Cunningham's interest in antiquities and numismatics was boosted by the activities of Jean Baptiste Ventura, an Italian general serving in Maharaja Ranjit Singh's court. Ventura, who was also an amateur archaeologist, frequently undertook excavations of Buddhist stupas in and around the domain of Ranjit Singh. In the process, he had unearthed large numbers of Bactrian, Greek and Kushan coins. Ventura had sent his findings to the Asiatic Society of Bengal in Calcutta.

At that time, the Company's currency system was about to be overhauled and Prinsep had sent out a request for coins and inscriptions from all over India. He was soon flooded with ancient coins, particularly from Punjab and Afghanistan. This fired Cunningham's interest in ancient coins. Cunningham not only supplied him with coins but also prepared an appendix to Prinsep's article on the relics in the Manikyala Stupa published in the 'Journal of the Asiatic Society of Bengal'.

In December 1834, while still in the army, Cunningham undertook another major project. At his own expense, he conducted an examination of the Dharmarajika and Chaukhandi mound in Sarnath. However, his most exciting excavation was that of the massive Dhameka Stupa, believed to be the place where Lord Buddha gave his first sermon. Here he found a stone slab inscribed with the Buddhist doctrine and also explored a monastery and a temple to the north of the stupa. The large collection of images and bas-reliefs found there were later presented to the Asiatic Society of Bengal. They are now housed in the Indian Museum in Kolkata.

However, the excavation was followed by unredeemable devastation. This incident is also referred to by Reverend M.A. Sherring, a Christian priest and Indologist, in his book, *The Sacred City of the Hindus*. He pointed out that,

> [I]n the erection of one of the bridges over the river Barna, forty-eight statues...were removed from Sárnáth and thrown into the river, to serve as a breakwater to the piers; and that, in the erection of the second bridge, the iron one, from fifty to sixty cart-loads of stones from Sárnáth were employed.

Although Cunningham was not responsible for this, the devastation was a direct fallout of the excavation.

In 1842, Cunningham located the ancient city of Sanskissa near Farrukhabad in present-day Uttar Pradesh. It had been mentioned by the Chinese pilgrim Faxian, who had carried out explorations there. Sanskissa was one of the most famous places of Buddhist pilgrimage, as it was here that the Buddha was believed to have descended from Heaven on a ladder made of gold and gems, accompanied by Indra and Brahma.

Next, Cunningham decided to embark on an excavation trip to Sanchi. His elder brother Joseph was a political agent at Bhopal, near Sanchi, giving him a great opportunity for this exploration that he didn't wish to miss. Cunningham reached Sanchi with his colleague Captain F.C. Maisey in 1851, and began excavations of the numerous Buddhist structures, mainly stupas built between the third century BCE and the sixth to seventh centuries CE.

Their most exciting discovery happened a few yards away from the main stupa. Cunningham began the excavation from the summit by sinking a shaft in the centre. In the inner chamber of the stupa, he found a large stone slab. Beneath the slab he discovered two stone boxes. Inside each box there was a relic casket and inside each casket were fragments of bones and beads. The boxes were engraved in Brahmi. Upon investigation, it was found that one of the boxes bore the name of Sariputra and the other, of Maha-Mogalannasa. These were two of the most famous disciples of the Buddha.

John Keay writes in his book, *India Discovered*, that finding the relics caskets would have given Cunningham the same thrill as the discovery of the 'graves of Saints Peter and Paul'. Cunningham was euphoric at discovering secrets undisturbed for two millennia. After this momentous discovery, Sanchi, which centuries before had slipped from Buddhist memory, again became a place of Buddhist pilgrimage. Cunningham recorded his findings in a book titled *The Bhilsa Topes.*

However, Cunningham and Maisey were inadvertently guilty of destroying important archaeological evidence. In their haste, they did not think it necessary to repair the massive breaches that shafting had created in the stupas. Following the excavation, the site of the stupas at Sanchi become a hunting ground for treasure-seekers and amateur archaeologists, who in their efforts to probe its hidden secrets caused irreparable damage to most of the structure. Though Cunningham and Maisey had recovered priceless relic caskets and other items, they also unwittingly contributed to the site being ruined.

The indictment came thirty years later, in 1881, from Sir Lepel Griffin, agent of the governor-general who was serving in central India. Griffin commented in his book *Famous Monuments of Central India*, 'a thousand years of time and weather have not done so much injury to the invaluable Stupas at Sanchi as was caused by the action of Alexander Cunningham who years ago mined deep into the topes... and never filled in his excavations.' However, one must keep in mind the fact that in those days modern methods of scientific excavations were unknown, and such diggings were a common practice in other parts of the world as well.

In the same year, Cunningham wrote to Col Sykes, the then chairman of the East India Company proposing the setting up of an archaeological survey in India. This was no doubt a commendable proposal, but his in the proposal has been criticized in many quarters. According to his communication, the need for an archaeological survey was not to understand India's past, but rather as a tool for 'the establishment of the Christian religion in India'. This was indeed a very strange justification for setting up an archaeological survey in a country!

In his defence, Cunningham was perhaps using a justification that he believed was more likely to procure the funding needed for the project. Regardless, Cunningham's proposal had to wait, as major upheavals were ongoing in the Company. Following the Great Rebellion of 1857, the rule of the British East India Company was transferred directly to the Crown, and Queen Victoria was proclaimed Empress of India.

On 30 June 1861, Cunningham retired from the army at the age of 47 after 28 years of continuous service. Following his retirement, he had more time in hand to pursue his interest in archaeology. During his tours of India, he had become deeply concerned by the sad state of neglect in which he found many of the historic ancient monuments of the country and decided to do something about it.

In November 1861, Cunningham had the chance to meet Lord Canning, then viceroy of India, in Allahabad. The meeting was about the former's proposal for the investigation of ancient remains in northern India. He took this opportunity to address a memorandum to Lord Canning in which he referred to the apathy of the colonial government towards the antiquities of India. In the first volume of *Four Reports Made During the Years 1862-63-64-65*, Cunningham made an impassioned plea for the preservation of India's ancient monuments, which, due to the almost total absence of any written history, formed 'the only reliable source of information as to the early condition of the country'.

Cunningham pointed out that the government had been chiefly occupied with the extension and consolidation of the empire, and during 100 years of British dominion, had done little for the preservation of India's ancient monuments. He predicted the likelihood of these monuments disappearing altogether in the near future 'unless preserved by the accurate drawings and faithful descriptions of the archaeologist.'

He also called attention to the fact that so far, 'All that has hitherto been done towards the illustration of ancient Indian history had been by the unaided efforts of private individuals.' Cunningham argued that initiating a careful and systematic investigation of all the existing monuments of ancient India would contribute greatly to the honour of the British government.

In the same memorandum, Cunningham proposed that, just as the Pliny the Elder, a roman author and natural philosopher, tried to understand the ancient geography of India by tracing the footsteps of Alexander the Great, he himself intended to follow in the footsteps of the Chinese pilgrim Hiuen Tsang (Xuanzang). In the seventh century, Xuanzang had travelled across India

> ...from west to east and back again for the purpose of visiting all the famous sites of Buddhist history and tradition, yet the numbers and appearance of the Brahmanical temples are also noted, and the travels of the Chinese pilgrim thus hold the same place in the history of India, which those of Pausannias hold in the history of Greece.

Cunningham's proposal resonated with Canning, who had recently toured northern India and had himself been struck by the neglect of the great mass of old buildings, and the way in which the ruins of a bygone civilization had been treated. Though Canning recognized that the investigations and maintenance of the principal antiquarian sites must now be an imperial responsibility, he suggested starting the project on a moderate scale. He proposed beginning with 'an accurate description... illustrated by plans, measurements, drawings or photographs, and by copies of inscriptions' of all those remains that 'most deserve notice, with the history of them so far as it may be traceable, and a record of the traditions that are retained regarding them.'

On 22 January 1862, Canning proposed that the work be entrusted to Cunningham, 'with the understanding that it continues during the present and the following cold season, by which time a fair judgment of its utility and interest may be formed. It may then be persevered in, and expanded, or otherwise dealt with as may seem good at the time.'

The minutes in the *Four Reports* also gave financial particulars and other details:

> Cunningham should receive Rs 450 a month, with Rs 250 when in the field to defray the cost of making surveys and measurements, and of other mechanical assistance. If something more should be necessary to obtain the services of a native subordinate of the Medical or Public Works Department, competent to take photographic views, it should be given.

The proposal was sanctioned by the colonial government and Lord Canning issued orders for the appointment of Cunningham as the director of the survey. This was one of his first acts since peace had been restored in the country after the cataclysm of the Great Rebellion. Thus, the Archaeological Survey of India began in 1862, with the appointment of Alexander Cunningham as the first archaeological surveyor.

Cunningham's attention was initially focused on surveying areas from Gaya in the east to the Indus in the northwest, and from Kalsi in the north to the Narmada in the south. His plan was to trace the Buddhist monuments from the accounts of Chinese pilgrims. What made his job easier was that the detailed accounts of the travels of the two Chinese monks Faxian and Xuanzang had become accessible to Western scholars, as they had been translated for the first time into French. The earliest translation of Faxian's autobiographical account in French was by Jean Pierre Abel Rémusat published in Paris in 1836. The French text was translated into English with additional notes by J.W. Laidley under the title *The Pilgrimage of Fa Hian*, published in Calcutta in 1848. Another well-known translation of Faxians texts into English was by James Legge published in 1886.

Of all the Chinese Buddhist pilgrims who came to India, Xuanzang had travelled the furthest. From about 630 CE to 645 CE, he had visited Buddhist holy places, collecting manuscripts and mapping out the whole of Buddhist India, including Punjab, Kashmir, Bihar, Assam and the Deccan peninsula.

Twelve hundred years later, Cunningham began his attempt to trace the monk's footsteps. From Xuanzang's travelogue, he could understand about the monasteries the Chinese pilgrim had visited, and about the monks who had lived there. Cunningham continued his efforts for four years, but the department was abolished by Lord Lawrence in 1866 and the survey came to an end. Thereafter, Cunningham left for England.

Four years later, the Duke of Argyll became the new secretary of state for India. He took up the archaeological matter again. In his dispatch of 11 January 1870 quoted in *Ancient India* published in 1953, he advised the colonial government to make a new start at establishing 'a central department which would tackle the archaeological problem of the entire country'. He also took the opportunity to vehemently denounce the prevailing tendency to rifle archaeological sites for their antiquities, laying special stress on the need for conservation, pointing out that it was the duty of the government to prevent the wanton acceleration of the decay of monuments.

Lord Mayo, then viceroy and governor-general, welcomed the proposal. On 30 May 1870, he said, as quoted by Upinder Singh in *The Discovery of Ancient India*:

> The duty of investigating, describing and protecting the ancient monuments of a country is recognized and acted on by every civilized nation in the world. India has done less in this direction than almost any other nation, and considering the vast materials for the illustration of history which lie unexplored in every part of Hindoostan, I am strongly of opinion that immediate steps should be taken for the creation under the Government of India of a machinery for discharging a duty, at once so obvious and so interesting.

Consequently, the Archaeological Survey of India was revived as a distinct department of the government, with a director-general as its head. Cunningham was appointed as the first director-general and assigned the following task, as quoted in *Ancient India*: 'A complete search over the whole country, and a systematic record and description of all architectural and other remains that are either remarkable for their antiquity, or their beauty, or their historical interest.'

Cunningham was further advised to summarize the work of former investigators and their results. He was also required to guide present and future researches. Cunningham's reports were printed by the government, but without the plans, drawings and photographs which ought to have been included. It was only in 1871 that these were reprinted with 40 small maps and 59 other drawings added.

Cunningham was assisted in his archaeological excavation and recording by J.D. Beglar, A.C.L. Carlleyle and H.B.W.

Garrick. Between 1872 and 1885, they toured the entire northern belt, including Central Provinces, Bundelkhand, Malwa, Bengal, Bihar and Rajputana, and their reports were collected in 23 volumes.

Cunningham summed up the work done by him as follows, quoted in *Indian Monuments* by N.S. Ramaswami:

> I have identified the sites of many of the chief cities and most famous places of ancient India, such as the rock of Aornos, the city of Taxila and the fortress of Sangala, all connected with the history of Alexander the Great. In India I have found the sites of the celebrated cities of Sanskisa, Sravasti and Kausambi, all immediately connected with the history of the Buddha. Among other discoveries I may mention the Great Stupa of Bharhut on which most of the principal events of the Buddha's life were sculptured and inscribed. I have found three dated inscriptions of King Ashoka, and my assistants have brought to light a new pillar of Ashoka, and a new text of his rock edicts in Bactrian characters, in which whole of the 12th edict, which is wanting in Shahbazgarhi text, is complete. I have traced the Gupta style of architecture in the temples of the Gupta Kings at Tigowa, Bilsar, Bhitargaon and Deogarh, and I have discovered new inscriptions of this powerful dynasty at Eran, Udayagiri and other places.

However, this list is incomplete, and does not include a number of other projects undertaken by him later.

Harappa in the Punjab had attracted Cunningham's attention early in 1853, when he was stationed at Multan. Though he had visited the site again three years later, it was only in 1872 that he made his first excavation. His chief discoveries in Harappa consisted of a number of stone implements for scraping wood or leather, numerous specimens of ancient pottery and a seal that was found along with two small objects resembling chess pawns. He described the seal as 'a smooth black stone without polish', and goes on to say, as recorded in volume five of the *Archaeological Survey of India*,

> The most curious object discovered at Harappa is a seal, ... On it is engraved very deeply a bull, without a hump, looking to the right, with two stars under the neck. Above the bull there is an inscription in six characters, which are quite unknown to me. They are certainly not Indian letters; and as the bull which accompanies them is without a hump, I conclude that the seal is foreign to India.

What an incredible miss! Cunningham thus lost a great opportunity of being hailed as the discoverer of the protohistoric civilization of the Indus Valley. It is difficult to understand how an archaeologist of Cunningham's stature could fail to recognize the remains of a great protohistoric civilization or even show any interest in further investigation.

In 1874, Cunningham submitted a proposal recommending that all ancient buildings not in living worship should be placed under the charge of the government. This was the foundation for the idea of designated national monuments. Then viceroy Lord Lytton took the initiative to secure India's architectural legacy by proposing the setting up of a post of 'curator of ancient monuments'. The proposal fructified during the administration of the next viceroy, Lord Ripon.

Cunningham was also a keen student of epigraphy, and was the prime mover behind the publication of *Corpus Inscriptionum Indicarum* in 1877. The book presented collected epigraphic material in a compact and handy volume, including a collection of edicts from Ashokan inscriptions. On Cunningham's behest, a separate post of government epigraphist was created in 1883. J.F. Fleet was the first appointee to the post.

Cunningham retired from the Archaeological Survey of India on 30 September 1885, returning to London to continue his research and writing. He had, by then, become an eminent authority on numismatics, but sold his collection of coins to the British Museum. Cunningham's last book was a beautifully illustrated volume on Mahabodhi, the great Buddhist temple near Gaya. The book was titled *Mahâbodhi: or the Great Buddhist Temple under the Bodhi Tree at Buddha-Gaya* and published in 1892.

Alexander Cunningham died at South Kensington on 28 November 1893 and was buried at Kensal Green Cemetery, London.

So, what is Alexander Cunningham's true place in Indian archaeology? Are we to accept Lord Canning's judgment of Cunningham, which declared him to be the man who had 'more than any other officer on this side of India, made the antiquities of the country his study' noted in the first volume of the *Archaeological Study of India*? Or do we believe F.S. Growse, who was unrelenting in his criticism, referring to Cunningham's reports as 'a trivial narrative and the crudest theories, in which the absence of critical and historical sense exceed all acceptable limits', as quoted by Ramaswamy?

According to former assistant director of national archives S.N. Roy, Cunningham's contribution to the development of Indian archaeology has been vigorously disputed. To many,

Cunningham was only a remarkable amateur whose reputation derived from the astonishing value and interest of his finds, and who remained to the last ignorant of scientific methods of archaeology. For him, archaeology was but a search for the past architectural styles, art treasures, coins and inscriptions. However, for many others, as mentioned in *Ancient India*, Cunningham was 'the father of Indian archaeology, who had by his ceaseless labour, given form and precision to aims and methods which had before him been only hazy and elusive'.

Despite all the criticism heaped on him, it cannot be denied that Cunningham remains one of the most important, if not the greatest, names associated with Indian archaeology. He was among the first to realize the necessity for organizing a countrywide survey of archaeological remains, and had, as early as 1848, pleaded the case for such a survey in an article titled 'Proposed Archaeological Investigations' published in the Asiatic Society's journal. Cunningham's investigations in central India with Maisey forms the first serious attempt to reconstruct the history of Buddhism from its architectural remains.

Cunningham's legacy can be summed up in the words of Dr Yojana Bhagat, coordinator at the department of Pali, Mumbai University, quoted by *Firstpost*:

> We have to be grateful for what he (Cunningham) has done for not just history and archaeology but for almost every branch of studies on India's history. Thanks to Cunningham, we have no confusion regarding the names of important historical sites in India. Since he was interested in Pali literature, he was able to identify even minor sites such as a river in Kosambi.

To quote Kurush Dalal's article in *Live History India*, 'He (Cunningham) left behind a legacy that is still unmatched in the subcontinent, not only in the astonishing discoveries he made but in the course he charted for Indian archaeologists. And, for this, we are ever indebted.'

14

VINCENT ARTHUR SMITH

Presenting the First Connected Narrative of Ancient India

'Until a hundred years ago, the recognizable structure of Indian history resembled a palace in ruins. The foundations were obscure, there were hardly any portion which was in fine preservation, mostly it was crumbling and all of it was overlain with rubble and weeds. Among the band of brilliant and tenacious scholars who worked to restore the palace, one of the most distinguished was Vincent Smith.'

– *Statesman*, May 1958

1904

VINCENT ARTHUR SMITH'S SEMINAL WORK *THE EARLY HISTORY of India from 600 B.C. to the Muhammadan Conquest, including the Invasion of Alexander The Great* had just been published. Writing a book on the early history of India had not been easy. Smith had been fully aware of the hazards of treading into uncharted territory but the hope that had sustained him throughout was his explicit belief, written in *The Early History*, that

> ...an orderly presentation of the ascertained facts of ancient Indian history may be of interest to a larger circle than that of professed orientalists, and that, as the subject becomes more familiar to the reading public, it will be found no less worthy of attention than better known departments of historical study.

Smith had assumed that the book would be of limited interest, mainly attracting orientalists and serious students of history. However, the book earned international fame and was recognized as a landmark work. By 1914, it had already been reprinted twice.

To really understand the difficulties faced by any historian attempting to write about early India in the nineteenth century, one has to study the period when William Jones had arrived in India. It was a time when the history of pre-Mughal India had been all but forgotten, and despite the groundbreaking work done by Jones, very little was known about India's past. At that time, the names of even the greatest monarchs of ancient India were unfamiliar to the general public.

According to British historian Mountstuart Elphinstone, another roadblock in writing about the history of ancient India was that no date in Indian history prior to Alexander's invasion could be determined with absolute precision. However, by the time Smith arrived on the scene, a lot of progress had been made in the recovery of the lost history of India, and a lot more information was forthcoming.

As acknowledged by Smith in the preface of *The Early History*, it had been easier for him to write about that period because, in the last seventy years, 'The researches of a multitude of scholars working in various fields have disclosed an unexpected wealth of materials for the reconstruction of ancient Indian history'. Thus, the necessary preliminary studies had already been carried out and Smith had at his disposal a huge and ever-growing store of knowledge to work with.

Despite its tremendous success, there remained some gaps in the first edition of *The Early History*. When Smith had begun writing the book, epigraphic evidence had been established for only two periods: the age of Ashoka and of the Guptas. There was no clarity yet on the period of the Scythians, the Parthians and the Kushanas, since the testimony of Greek writers and Chinese travellers related to only certain restricted periods of time. Once more information about these periods were available, Smith was able to rectify some omissions in the second edition.

By the time Smith began work on the third edition of *The Early History,* a huge amount of new matter and fresh discussion had accumulated. This made it necessary to rework large chunks of the book and created another problem: if Smith were to include all the new information, he would need to add another volume. But he rejected the idea as he wished to stick to his decision to 'confine the book within the limits of a single volume of reasonable size and moderate price.'

Smith had stated that his aim in writing the book was to 'present the story of ancient India, ...in the form of a connective narrative, based upon the most authentic evidence available; to relate facts... with impartiality... and to discuss the problem of history in a judicial spirit.' And, despite all the roadblocks faced by Smith, he succeeded beyond expectation.

What made *The Early History* stand out from any other history of India published till then was that, for the first time, the chronology was based on sound evidence. For Smith, the book was primarily a political history, and he strongly believed that the ancient Indian political history was significant and important in its own right.

The last of the Orientalists, Vincent Smith was born on June 3, 1848 in Dublin. He was the fifth son of Aquilla Smith and his wife Esther. The senior Smith was a prominent doctor, who was also a numismatist and an amateur archaeologist.

Smith's love of history began early. A brilliant student, he took up the study of classics, history and English literature in Trinity College, Dublin. After which he sat for the Indian Civil Service examination at the age of 21 and was allowed to choose where he wanted to serve in India due to his high grades. So, Smith chose to be allotted to the North-Western Provinces (now Uttar Pradesh). Before joining, he had to undergo a period of probation of two years, studying law and oriental languages. He arrived in India in 1871.

Smith began his career in Ghazipur, a district in the North-Western Provinces, as an assistant magistrate and collector. In 1881, he wrote a guidebook for the staff of that department titled *The Settlement Officer's Manual for the North-Western Provinces*. The book detailed the functions of the staff with pithy instructions such as: 'The settlement officer should remember that he is a land valuer, not a mineralogist.'

Over time, the guidebook became a useful reference for the settlement officers of the province.

Smith worked in India from 1871 to 1900, serving in a variety of magisterial and executive positions in the North-Western Provinces. However, not much is known about his personal life except that he married Mary Elizabeth Tute during this period, and had three sons and one daughter with her.

Smith had come to India at a time when the memories of the uprising of 1857 were still fresh in the people's minds. And Bundelkhand had suffered badly during the revolt. Smith's historical curiosity lead him to study the documents relating to the revolt, which ignited his interest in the art and architecture of India. It soon developed into an absorbing interest in every aspect of Indian history. He began research on the history and archaeology of the districts of Bundelkhand, a passion that would continue for the rest of his life.

Smith's detailed writings on the history, customs, and folklore of the area in and around Bundelkhand were published in the 'Journal of the Bengal Asiatic Society' in 1875, 1877 and 1881. He also wrote a paper on two copper plates found at Nanaura, a village in the district Banda in the then North-Western Provinces, from the Chandela period – the Chandela kings belonged to an Indian Rajput clan who ruled over a large part of Bundelkhand in central India from the ninth century to the thirteenth century.

Besides history and archaeology, Smith was also fascinated with numismatics, an interest which he had acquired from his father in childhood. It became a full-blown passion after his arrival in India. It wasn't long before he decided to take on the project of re-cataloguing thousands of coins at the Indian Museum in Calcutta. He was now being hailed as the leading authority on the coinage of the Gupta period.

Apart from this, Smith had also been deeply influenced by Sir Alexander Cunningham's research on Indian Buddhist temples. He had begun collecting manuscripts and studying monuments and archaeological remains. However, it was only after his appointment as joint magistrate of Basti district in Uttar Pradesh in 1885 that he began a serious study of the path traversed by Faxian and Xuanzang during their travels in India. Smith began to gather more information about India's past and soon became an expert on Buddhist history.

After having put in thirty years in the Indian Civil Service, Smith wanted to step away from bureaucratic duties and spend more time in scholastic work. This led him to leave India in July 1900.

On his return to Britain, Smith was appointed as reader in Indian history and Hindustani at the University of Dublin. In 1910, he moved to St. John's College, Oxford, as reader in Indian history and curator of the Indian Institute. During his time in Oxford, he wrote and published frequently and soon earned global fame as an expert Sanskritist and a scholar of Indian history. He contributed numerous articles in leading journals both in England and abroad.

Smith had been preparing an index for Cunningham's Journal of the Archaeological Survey of India. While working on the indexing, he was able to gather material that would lead to the first biography of Ashoka. The book on Ashoka was intended to be the first of the *Rulers of India* series by Professor

Rhys Davids, a scholar of Pali Buddhism. Unfortunately, that did not happen, and Smith took over with the approval of Davids. *Asoka, the Buddhist Emperor of India* was published in 1901, soon after his return to Dublin.

In this book, Smith's focus was on keeping the legends separate from authentic history. A second edition came out in 1909 and a third was in the works at the time of Smith's death in 1920. *Asoka* later became a part of *Early History*. A fourth edition of the latter book was published in 1924, four years after the author's death. It had been revised by S.M. Edwardes of the Indian Civil Service.

Smith's next book was *A History of Fine Art in India and Ceylon*, published in 1911. Since it came out a year after the publication of the revised edition of James Fergusson's *A History of Indian and Eastern Architecture*, historians view *A History of Fine Art* more as a supplement to Fergusson's great work.

To quote R. Vajreswari's 1966 *Handbook*, Smith's biographies had been about the strong and successful: 'Chandragupta Maurya, "a man of blood and iron"; Ashoka, "a masterful autocrat ruling church and state alike with a strong hand"; and Samudra Gupta, the "Indian Napoleon".' Thus, it was no surprise when Smith's next book was about Akbar. The book was titled *Akbar, the Great Mogul* and published in 1917. In the preface, Smith mentions that the idea had come to him 24 years earlier when he was editing *The Rambles and Recollections of an Indian Official* by Sir William Sleeman.

Smith had been strongly influenced by Sleeman's comment that, as quoted in his Akbar the *Great Mogul, 1542-*

1605, 'Akbar has always appeared to me among sovereigns what Shakespeare was among poets'. While writing this book, Smith consulted *The Commentary of Father Monserrate: S.J., on his Journey to the Court of Akbar* (translated from the original Latin) as well as other writings of early European travellers who had been to the Mughal court.

Following his own conviction that a comparatively brief biography enjoys many advantages over a voluminous history, Smith designed this book as a biography of Akbar rather than as a formal history. In his words, quoted by C.S. Srinivasachari in his chapter on Smith in *Eminent Orientalists*:

> He founded or at least re-founded the Mogul Empire which received from him life and vigour enough to endure as a great power for a century after his death. He had the broad views of a true far-seeing statesman and knew how to choose, use and keep loyal servants. His policy of impartial toleration was all his own. Personally, he was one of the most kingly of kings and his superlative qualities enabled him to keep a firm hand upon the sceptre even to the end. His aberrations must be viewed in proper perspective and should be regarded as only spots on the sun.

Interestingly, another Indian whom Smith wrote about is Tulsidas, the legendary Hindu poet-saint who had authored the great Hindu epic *Ramcharitmanas*, the most popular version of the Ramayana. In his masterful summary of Akbar, Smith refers to Tulsidas, who lived and wrote in the time of Akbar, as 'the tallest tree in the "magic garden" of medieval Hindu poesy.'

One of the lesser-known facts of Smith's career is about his relationship with Lord Curzon, who was at the time looking for a new director-general for the revamped Archaeological Survey of India. Smith was the natural choice for the post, and his name was strongly recommended by the India Office as 'an old India hand' with extensive administrative experience.

Nonetheless, his candidature did not find favour with Curzon, who said that his 'impression is that [Smith] is deficient in expert and artistic knowledge and in energy', as quoted by Nayanjot Lahiri in *Finding Forgotten Cities.* Perhaps Curzon was looking for a younger, more energetic man, but the main reason seems to have been his aversion to Smith's brand of scholarship, which he felt was 'colonial' in character.

However, being active in the Royal Asiatic Society, Smith became a member of its council in 1915. He was awarded the society's gold medal in 1918. The following year he was elected as the vice president of the society and awarded an honorary D.Litt. from the University of Dublin. He was also elected as fellow of the University of Allahabad.

Smith's last great work was *The Oxford History of India,* published in 1919. It narrates the history of the subcontinent from prehistoric times to the end of 1911. The book came in for a great deal of criticism as it had a pronounced bias toward British imperialism. This imperialistic bias could be seen in many derogatory and unsubstantiated comments such as 'Hindus are caste–ridden and therefore inefficient as a fighting force' or referring to Muslims as 'fanatics' and 'pests of humanity'. Fortunately, the book was corrected by a group of British scholars in a new edition that was released by the Oxford University Press in 1958.

Soon after the publication of *The Oxford History of India,* Smith's health began to fail.Vincent Arthur Smith passed away at Oxford on 6 February 1920.While many of his judgments may seem simplistic in light of modern historical research, he was a pioneer of Indian history.

15

SIR JOHN HUBERT MARSHALL

The Man Who Left India 3,000 Years Older

'Hitherto India has almost universally been regarded as one of the younger countries of the world... Now, at a single bound, we have taken back our knowledge of Indian civilization some 3,000 years earlier and have established the fact that in the third millennium before Christ, and even before that, the peoples of the Punjab and Sind were living in well-built cities and were in possession of a relatively mature culture with a high standard of art and craftsmanship and a developed system of pictographic writing.'

– Sir John Hubert Marshall in *Revealing India's Past*, 1939[1]

February 1902, Calcutta

IT WAS A VERY SPECIAL DAY IN THE LIFE OF JOHN HUBERT Marshall. Just one month before his 26th birthday, he had taken over as the Director-General of Archaeology in India!

---

[1] Marshall's statement about the existence of a prehistoric civilization in India (following the discovery of artefacts recovered from Harappa and Mohenjodaro).

What made it even more special for him was that he had been handpicked by the Viceroy and Governor-General Lord Curzon himself, for the post of director-general of the Archaeological Survey of India. And he had been given the responsibility of conducting archaeological excavations at Taxila, an ancient bustling city of ancient India. It was a city that had been almost wiped out of people's memories until Alexander Cunningham established that the modern township Saraikhala was the site of ancient Takshashila. The name had been shortened by Greek writers to Taxila. The site is now a city in modern-day Pakistan.

However, after carrying out preliminary excavations in and around the region, Cunningham had not taken it further. Thus, it fell upon Marshall to expand on Cunningham's work. He renewed excavations of the site in 1913, trying to dig out the hidden secrets of the ancient town. Soon, he uncovered ancient jewellery and domestic artefacts in the area. Marshall was captivated by the antiquity of the region and its variegated history.

Although there was no recorded history of Taxila, it had been referred to in different eras in various literary accounts of ancient India, including ancient Indian mythologies. The earliest mention of 'Takshashila' was in the Ramayana. It was named after its founder, the prince Taksha, who was the son of Bharata, a brother of Rama. It is also believed that the Mahabharata was first recited at Taxila during the grand snake sacrifice by King Janamejaya.

We next hear of Taxila in the Jatakas, where it is referred to as a great centre of learning. From the accounts of the Chinese travellers, it would appear that the city was at the height of its prosperity when Faxian visited it at the beginning of the fifth century CE. Taxila remained a flourishing hub of Buddhist sanctuaries and monasteries till it was invaded and sacked by the Huns. By the time Xuanzang visited the region in the seventh century CE, Taxila lay deserted. The once thriving city was in ruins. After that, there was no mention of the city.

For Marshall, Taxila was just the first of his many spectacular discoveries that ultimately helped provide evidence of the antiquity of India. Marshall was passionate about archaeology, but all his zeal and dedication would have come to naught if destiny, in the form of Lord Curzon, had not intervened.

Lord Curzon served as viceroy in India from 1899 to 1905. Indian archaeology can be divided roughly into two equal but distinct phases: the period which preceded Lord Curzon's Indian stint, and the period that followed. The pre-Curzon period did have some lucky finds but there was no systematic approach; as a result, excavations were incomplete and restorations awkward. This was mainly due to the apathy of the colonial government then. Cunningham was the archaeological protagonist in the first period.

In the post-Curzon period, John Marshall became the main figure. The Curzon/Marshall alliance has been hailed by scholars as the most fruitful association in the annals of archaeology. Leading scholar G.N. Das says in his 1959 essay on Marshall, 'If Lord Curzon was the greatest patron and champion Indian archaeology ever had, John Marshall was certainly one of its major architects.'

John Marshall was the youngest of four sons born to Fredrick Marshall and his first wife, Annie Evans. He was born in Chester, England on 19 March 1876. John began his education at Dulwich in London, and later joined King's College at Cambridge, where he studied Classical Tripos. While at Cambridge, Marshall was inspired to go to Greece and study Greek archaeology. He enrolled himself in the British School at Athens in 1898, and participated in archaeological operations not only in Greece but also in Crete and Turkey.

Marshall arrived in India after he was appointed as director-general of the Archaeological Survey of India. But why was he selected for this position despite still being very young? It all began when Lord Curzon became viceroy, and then governor-general, of India. At that time, the Archaeological Survey of India was languishing without leadership since the colonial government's decision that there was no requirement for a director-general of archaeology. However, Lord Curzon had a great admiration for Indian civilization, and thought that India boasted of 'the most glorious galaxy of monuments in the world', as quoted by John Keay in his book *India Discovered*. Soon after arriving in India, Curzon visited Ellora, Agra and Fatehpur Sikri, among other sites. He understood the need to preserve the historical monuments there, and requested the government back home to appoint a director of archaeology.

Curzon was on good terms with Lord George Hamilton, then secretary of state. In 1901, Curzon wrote to Hamilton, as noted by L.J.L Dundas in his 1928 biography of Lord Curzon:

> Do let me entreat you to save from their (the India

> Council's) devastating and pernicious activity the proposals which we are sending home to you this week for appointing a director or inspector-general of archaeology and for spending a little more money for a few years on the conservation of ancient buildings.

The following year, his plea was accepted, and Vincent Arthur Smith was nominated for the position. However, Curzon preferred a younger man who had distinguished himself as a scholar at one of the English universities and who had experience in archaeological work in Greece, Egypt or Asia Minor (that is, present-day Turkey).

A search was mounted for a suitable person, with the director of the British Museum joining the selection process. In the end, John Marshall of King's College, Cambridge was appointed for a period of five years, at just 25 years old! Curzon's impression about Marshall can be understood from a letter recorded in *Finding Forgotten Cities* by Nayanjot Lahiri. He wrote to Hamilton at this time saying, 'I made his (Marshall's) acquaintance before leaving Calcutta, and thought him rather distinguished in appearance and quite becomingly keen. I told him that he must learn Sanskrit at once, in order to be able to deal with inscriptions, one of the most important branches of Indian archaeology.'

Before leaving for India, Marshall married Florence Longhurst. He arrived in India on 22 February 1902 and began work as the director-general of the Archaeological Survey of India. Initially, his chief tasks were the excavation, preservation and repair of ancient Indian monuments, temples, sculptures and paintings that were in a sad state of decay as a result of centuries of neglect. Das mentions that Marshall was also given the responsibility to ensure 'that the ancient monuments of the country are properly cared for, that they are not utilized for the purpose which are inappropriate or unseemly, that repairs are executed when required and that any restorations, which may be attempted, are conducted on artistic lines'.

He was also tasked with a general supervision over all archaeological work in the country, 'whether it be that of excavation, or preservation, or repair, or of the registration and description of monuments and ancient remains'. Marshall had to assist the provincial administrations in ascertaining and formulating the special requirements of each province, and was also expected to submit an annual report on the progress that year.

Marshall began with the reorganization of the department, and then started to explore and study ancient remains and buried sites to copy inscriptions. Considering the vast size and diversity of India, the task was indeed formidable. It was made even more difficult by the miniscule resources allotted for the department of archaeology.

Around that time, archaeology was introduced as a subject in Indian universities for the first time. The first Indians to win scholarships to study archaeology were Daya Ram Sahni and Ghulam Yazdani. The former would eventually become a director-general of the Archaeological Survey of India, and the latter, director of archaeology in the Nizam's territory. Marshall oversaw repairs of many historic buildings in Delhi, such as the Quwaat-ul-Islam mosque, the Qila Kuhna mosque, the tomb of Tughlak Shah and the mausoleum of Humayun. The job was carried out with such skill and ingenuity that

Curzon declared that the neglected and half-collapsed ruins were made as perfect as the day they were built.

Next, Marshall's focus shifted to the conservation and maintenance of the monuments in Agra, where he put into operation the innovative schemes of conservation initiated by Curzon. He recreated the original landscape of the Taj Mahal, transforming the inhospitable wastelands of the surrounding areas into beautiful gardens. Every building in the garden enclosure was meticulously repaired, and the discovery of old plans helped them in restoring the garden's water channels and flowerbeds exactly to their original state.

The work done by Marshall and his team at Agra so impressed the viceroy that he wrote to the secretary of state, as found in *Lord Curzon in India* published in 1906:

> It (the Taj Mahal) is no longer approached through dusty wastes and a squalid bazaar. A beautiful park takes their place; and the group of mosques and tombs, the arcaded streets and grassy courts that precede the main building are once more as nearly as possible what they were when completed by the masons of Shah Jahan.

Among other projects, Shah Jahan's pavilion on the Anna Sagar lake in Ajmer was restored to its pristine beauty, and the modern offices and bungalows built on the site were demolished. In the same city, Arhai Din ka Jhonpra mosque – one of the earliest and most magnificent of Indian mosques – was also repaired.

Marshall then restored the Tower of Fame (*Kirti Stambha*) in Chittorgarh, a splendid group of monuments in Mandu and the temples of Khajuraho. Other repair work included the brick monuments of Gaur and Pandua, which were capitals of the independent sultans of Bengal, the Konark temple, the Adil Shahi monuments in Bijapur and the ruins of Vijaynagar.

Marshall's task was made more difficult by the callous attitude of the colonial government. He was shocked to find that civil and military offices had been allowed to take over many of the ancient monuments. At Ahmedabad, the mosque of Sidi-Sayid – which had pierced-stone lattice work and demilune windows – was used as a *tehsildar's kutcherry* and was disfigured by partitions and whitewash.[2] The lovely tiled Dai Anga mosque at Lahore had become the office for the North-Western Railway, and a post office and dak bungalow occupied a mosque in Bijapur.

Conservation work could be started only after evicting these government offices and other military establishments. However, the military authorities were not amenable to the entreaties of the provincial governments. The only person with the power to remove them was the viceroy. It was doubtful if anyone of a less forceful personality than Lord Curzon would have succeeded in dislodging the intruders. Walter Roper Lawrence, a private secretary to the viceroy, recalled in his 1928 book *The India We Served*, how in one of the ancient buildings they found a squalid post office, and Curzon indignantly 'ordered the whole staff to quit on the spot. This might have inconvenienced the postal deliveries for

---

[2] A tehsil is an administrative division or township within a district and the officer in charge is the tehsildar. A kutcherry is a court of law.

the day, but it evoked the conscience of the authorities and had its effect all over India'.

Lord Curzon then began a legislation for the protection of the ancient monuments and antiquities of the country. Its object was threefold: firstly, to ensure the proper upkeep and repair of ancient buildings in private ownership, excepting those that were being used for religious purposes; secondly, prevent excavation of sites of historic interest by ignorant and unauthorized persons; and finally, to control the trafficking of antiquities. A bill was drafted based on a similar legislation used in Italy and Greece, and modified to suit the circumstances in India. The Ancient Monuments Preservation Act was passed in 1904, providing 'for the preservation of ancient monuments, for the exercise of control over traffic in antiquities and over excavation in certain places, and for the protection and acquisition in certain cases of ancient monuments and of objects of archaeological, historical and artistic interest'.

The next step was to make the Archaeological Survey of India a permanent institution from its temporary five-year term that had started in 1899. In 1905, Marshall proposed the retention of the Archaeological Survey of India on a permanent basis. While forwarding the proposal, Marshall noted that, as quoted by Das: 'the work of the archaeological officers is of a kind which cannot be discharged by any other existing agency and it can only cease if the government cease to admit their responsibility for the preservation of the ancient remains of the country'.

His request was granted and the Archaeological Survey of India was transformed into a permanent body on 28 April

1906. A government epigraphist for India was also appointed. In 1914, Marshall was conferred a knighthood for his efforts.

In 1915, Marshall published a review of the progress and principles of archaeological work in India. On the policy of conservation, as noted by Das, Marshall wrote that the government understood

> ...the deplorable harm that may be done in the name of restoration, and, except in special circumstances, are opposed to its being undertaken. It is recognized, however, that there are considerations of a social, political and climatic character which must always be taken into account, and that in this country, in particular, it is impracticable to lay down one law which will be applicable to every case.

Marshall firmly believed that a distinction needed to be made between the older edifices, such as Buddhist, Hindu and Jain monuments, and the more modern constructions. In the case of temples, mosques, tombs or palaces where ceremonial functions were still being performed, it was felt that restoration work was sometimes not only desirable but justified, rather than those buildings that were just antiquarian relics. For him, the object was 'not to reproduce what has been defaced or destroyed, but to save what is left from further injury or decay, and to preserve it as a national heirloom for posterity.'

One of the reasons for Marshall's appointment as director-general of the Archaeological Survey of India was to introduce into the country the scientific methods of digging that had yielded brilliant results in Greece and Crete. The manner in which archaeological excavations were being carried out in India at the time was derisively referred to as the 'idol-digging method', as the excavations of historical sites were done more for collecting sculptures than for understanding civilizational evolution or the area's history.

Despite prioritizing restoration and preservation over excavation, Marshall thought it proper to familiarize his colleagues with the scientific method of digging. Some trial digging was done at Charsadda in the ancient site of valley of Peshawar, the ancient site of Pushkalavati on the Swat river. The question often asked is why he focused on well-known Buddhist sites and not the larger city sites, such as the Harappa mounds. Marshall explained, as noted by John Cumming in *Revealing India's Past*:

> We were at that time better informed – thanks to the Chinese pilgrims and the researches of earlier archaeologists – about these Buddhist monuments generally than about any other class of remains and we were more likely to get spectacular finds on these Buddhist sites. Such finds were absolutely indispensable to us if we were to interest the public in our work and secure more adequate funds for it.

In a blow for Marshall, Curzon left India in 1906. Marshall then turned his attention to the excavation of the early historic site of Taxila. He began work on the site in 1913, and the excavation occupied him for the next two decades. 'There can be few archaeologists now living who have devoted as many years to the excavation of a single site as I have devoted to Taxila,' Marshall wrote in his 1951 book entitled *Taxila*. 'The manifold discoveries made in the course of those twenty-two years have thrown a flood of new light on the political and religious history of the North-West and in many respects revolutionized our knowledge of its material culture during lengthy periods between 500 BC and AD 500'.

Marshall considered the Taxila excavation to be his best work, but many scholars rank his efforts at Sanchi higher. At the latter site, he successfully restored monuments that had been lying desolate for centuries. Marshall was of the view that 'the monuments of Sanchi are the noblest of all the monuments which early Buddhism has bequeathed to India', as he wrote in his *A Guide to Sanchi* published in 1918. But he also adds that these are monuments about which little information was available. He noted, 'Ancient Indian writers scarcely mention them; the Chinese pilgrims, who are such a mine of information regarding other Buddhist sites, pass by them in silence.'

The funds for the exploration and preservation of the Sanchi monuments were provided by the Begum of Bhopal. In 1940, Marshall wrote a book on Sanchi with his archaeologist friends A. Foucher and Nani Gopal Majumdar, and published it in three volumes. It remains the only definitive description of any great Indian historic site.

Alexander Cunningham had visited Harappa in 1872 and had described it as 'the most extensive of all the old sites along the banks of the Ravi' as quoted by Cumming. Strangely, no further notice was taken of the Harappan mounds for nearly four decades. It was only in 1914 that Marshall deputed a superintendent by the name of Harold Hargreaves, an archaeologist who went on to succeed Marshall, to Harappa for assessing the land to be acquired for excavation. After taking photographs of Harappa and some of its historical artefacts, Hargreaves recommended excavation in Harappa.

However, work could commence only after local zamindars were compensated for the mounds owned by them. The mounds were then brought under the protection of the Ancient Monuments Act. Digging began in 1921, supervised by another superintendent by the name of Daya Ram Sahni. More pictographic seals were found besides a large collection of pottery vessels. Sahni's excavations at Harappa established the existence of a civilization older than any ancient city hitherto known to exist within the Indian subcontinent. He published his report in 1922, establishing the prehistoric nature of the remains.

The work of excavation in Mohenjo-Daro started in December 1922 under a superintendent called R.D. Banerji. In Mohenjo-Daro, there were mounds of entombed relics of various ancient cultures piled on top of each other. Unlike Sahni, Banerji was not apprenticed as an excavator. However, he quickly understood after discovering a number of flint instruments that these sites in Sind, in modern-day Pakistan, were of immense antiquity, because they were marked by the presence of stone tools. Banerji dispatched his report to Marshall in 1926.

A close examination of artefacts and antiquities recovered from Harappa and Mohenjo-Daro left Marshall overwhelmed. As mentioned by Cummings, he was convinced that they 'belonged to the same stage of culture and approximately to the same age, and that they were totally distinct from anything previously known to us in India.' It was a moment not dissimilar to when the German researcher Heinrich Schliemann discovered the ancient city of Troy.

Once convinced of the significance of the discovery, Marshall made a public announcement in the *Illustrated London News* on 24 September 1924 that read:

> Not often has it been to archaeologists, as it was given to Schliemann at Tiryns and Mycenae, or to Stein in the deserts of Turkestan, to light upon the remains of a long-forgotten civilization. It looks, however, at this moment, as if we were on the threshold of such a discovery in the plains of the Indus.

This declaration is considered by many historians as the most famous statement about the Indus civilization. Thus, the antiquity of 'Indus Valley Civilization' was established. These discoveries were hailed by the scientific world and increased the prestige of the Archaeological Survey of India.

On 6 September 1928, Marshall retired from the post of director-general of the Archaeological Survey of India. However, he was re-employed and tasked with preparing pending reports on Taxila, Mandu, Delhi, Sanchi and Agra among others. Marshall's excavation methods were subsequently criticized by one of his successors, R.E. Mortimer Wheeler, but there is no doubt that Marshall succeeded significantly in the awakening of interest in India's past.

Marshall left India for good on 15 March 1934. However, he continued assisting his former employers in a special capacity till the end of that year. He was elected as Fellow of the British Academy in 1936. Sir John Hubert Marshall passed away at his home in Guildford, Avondale, England on 17 August 1958 at the age of 82.

Marshall's legacy can be found enshrined in his publications, such as *Indian Archaeological Policy* and *Conservation Manual: A Handbook for the Use of Archaeological Officers and Others Entrusted with the Care of Ancient Monuments*. His noteworthy contributions can mainly be seen in the detailed reporting of his fieldwork, which included both explorations and excavations. His reports on Mohenjo-Daro and the Indus civilisation, the monuments of Sanchi and the Taxila site, all reveal the capability of archaeological operations to reconstruct the past. John Hubert Marshall will be remembered for his discoveries about prehistoric civilization of India.

WORKS CITED

Chapter 1: Sir William Jones

A.J. Arberry, *Oriental Essays: Portraits of Seven Scholars (1960)*, United Kingdom: Taylor & Francis, 2016.

Asiatic Researches or Transactions of the Society Instituted in Bengal, for Inquiring into the History and Antiquities, the Arts, Sciences, and Literature, of Asia, 1788.

Garland Cannon, *A Biography Of Sir William Jones (1746-1794)*, 1960. http://archive.org/details/in.ernet.dli.2015.458887.

———. William Jones, *The Letters: Of Sir William Jones*, ed. Garland Cannon, Clarendon Press, 1970.

Centenary Review of the Asiatic Society of Bengal from 1784 to 1883, India: Thacker, Spink and Company, 1885.

Suniti Chaterji, 'Sir William Jones', in *Portraits of Linguists A Biographical Source Book for the History of Western Linguistics, 1746-1963*, ed. Thomas Albert Sebeok, vol. 1, Indiana: Indiana University Press, 1966. https://muse.jhu.edu/book/84741/

Franklin Edgerton, 'Sir William Jones', in *Portraits of Linguists A Biographical Source Book for the History of Western Linguistics,*

1746-1963, ed. Thomas Albert Sebeok, vol. 1, Indiana: Indiana University Press, 1966. https://muse.jhu.edu/book/84741/

William Jones, 'A Discourse on the Institution of a Society for Inquiring into the History, Civil and Natural, the Antiquities, Arts, Sciences and Literature, of Asia', ELIOHS, n.d., <http://www.eliohs.unifi.it/testi/700/jones/Preliminary_Discourse.html>.

———. 'The Tenth Anniversary Discourse, on Asiatick History, Civil and Natural, Delivered 28th February, 1793.', ELIOHS, <http://www.eliohs.unifi.it/testi/700/jones/Jones_Discourse_10.html>.

Marcus Junianus Justinus, Nepos Eutropius, Cornelius, *Justin, Cornelius Nepos, and Eutropius, literally translated, with notes and a general index,* trans. J.S. Watson, London: H.G. Bohn, 1853.

John Keay, *India Discovered: The Achievement of the British Raj*, Windward, 1981.

O.P. Kejariwal, *The Asiatic Society of Bengal and the Discovery of India's Past, 1784-1838*, New York: Oxford University Press, 1988.

David Kopf, *British Orientalism and the Bengal Renaissance: The Dynamics of Indian Modernization 1773-1835,* United States: University of California Press, 1969.

Henry Roscoe, *Lives of Eminent British Lawyers*, United States: Carey & Hart, 1841.

John Shore, *Memoirs of the Life, Writings and Correspondence, of Sir William Jones*, United Kingdom: Brettell, printer, 1806.

Chapter 2: Sir Charles Wilkins

Nathaniel Halhed, *A Grammar of the Bengal Language*, 1778.

'HALHED, Nathaniel Brassey (1751-1830), of West Square, Southwark, Surr', *History of Parliament Online*. Web. <https://

www.historyofparliamentonline.org/volume/1790-1820/member/halhed-nathaniel-brassey-1751-1830>.

Rajesh Kochhar, *Sanskrit and the British Empire*, India: Taylor & Francis, 2021.

K.S.S. Seshan, 'Charles Wilkins: He turned their gaze to Sanskrit', *the Hindu*, 13 December 2019. Web. <https://www.thehindu.com/society/history-and-culture/charles-wilkins-he-turned-their-gaze-to-sanskrit/article30298306.ece>

The Asiatic Annual Register: Or a View of the History of Hindustan and of the Politics, Commerce and Literature of Asia, Cadell and Davies, 1801.

Charles Wilkins, *A Grammar of the Sanskrĭta Language*, United Kingdom: Balmer, 1808.

———. *The Bhagavat-Geeta, Or, Dialogues of Kreeshna and Arjoon*, London: C. Nourse, 1785.

Chapter 3: Nathaniel Brassey Halhed

Anonymous review of *A Code of Gentoo Laws or Ordinations of the Pandits*, from *Critical Review*, XLIV. September 1777, 177–91.

John Buchanan, 'Buchanan's Travel's in the Mysore', *The Edinburgh Review Or Critical Journal*, vol. 12(25): 91, 1809.

Bernard S. Cohn, *Colonialism and its Forms of Knowledge: The British in India*, United Kingdom: Princeton University Press, 1996.

K.S. Diehl, 'Bengali Types and Their Founders', *The Journal of Asian Studies* Vol. 27, no. 2: 335–38, 1968. https://doi.org/10.2307/2051755.

G.W. Forrest, ed. *Selections from the State Papers of the Governors-general of India*. United Kingdom: B. H. Blackwell, 1910. <https://archive.org/details/selectionsfromst02forr/page/295/mode/1up>

M.J. Franklin, 'Cultural Possession, Imperial Control, and Comparative Religion: The Calcutta Perspectives of Sir William Jones and Nathaniel Brassey Halhed', *The Yearbook of English Studies*,Vol. 32:1–18, 2002.

Nathaniel Halhed, *A Code of Gentoo Laws, Or, Ordinations of the Pundits: From a Persian Translation, Made from the Original Written in the Shanscrit Language*, United Kingdom: 1776.

'HALHED, Nathaniel Brassey (1751-1830), of West Square, Southwark, Surr', *History of Parliament Online*, 2021. Web. <https://www.historyofparliamentonline.org/volume/1790-1820/member/halhed-nathaniel-brassey-1751-1830>.

John Johnston and Samuel Parr, *The Works of Samuel Parr: With Memoirs of his Life and Writings, and a Selection from His Correspondence,* United Kingdom: Longman, Rees, 1828.

Linda Kelly, *Richard Brinsley Sheridan: A Life*, United Kingdom: Faber & Faber, 2012.

William Robertson, *An Historical Disquisition Concerning the Knowledge which the Ancients Had of India:And the Progress of Trade with that Country Prior to the Discovery of the Passage to it by the Cape of Good Hope. With an Appendix, Containing Observations on the Civil Policy, the Laws and Judicial Proceedings, the Arts, the Sciences, and Religious Institutions, of the Indians*, United States: Harper, 1835.

Rosane Rocher, *Orientalism, Poetry, and the Millennium: The Checkered life of Nathaniel Brassey Halhed, 1751-1830*, India: Motilal Banarsidass, 1983.

Felix Seddon, *An Address Delivered in King's College, London, Introductory to a Course of Lectures on the Languages and Literature of Asia*, 1835

The Asiatic Journal and Monthly Register for British and Foreign India, China, and Australia, United Kingdom: Parbury, Allen, and Company, 1828.

Chapter 4: James Prinsep

Centenary Review of the Asiatic Society of Bengal from 1784 to 1883, India: Thacker, Spink and Company, 1885.

H.E.A Cotton, *Calcutta, Old and New: A Historical and Descriptive Handbook to the City*, ed. N.R. Ray, India: General Printers & Publishers, 1950.

Charles Allen, *The Buddha and the Sahibs*, United Kingdom: John Murray Press, 2015.

'A tribute to the founder of modern Varanasi - James Prinsep', *TwoCircles.net,* 9 September 2009. Web. <http://twocircles.net/2009sep08/tribute_founder_modern_varanasi_james_prinsep.html>.

John Cumming, ed. *Revealing India's Past*, Kiribati: India Society, 1939.

Dictionary of National Biography. United Kingdom: Oxford University Press, 1901.

'Feroz Shah Kotla', *Delhi Information.* Web. <https://www.delhiinformation.in/tourism/monuments/ferozshahkotla.html>.

Journal of the Asiatic Society of Bengal, Vol. 1, India: 1832.

Journal of the Asiatic Society of Bengal, Vol. 6, India: 1837.

O.P. Kejariwal, *The Asiatic Society of Bengal and the Discovery of India's Past,* Delhi: Oxford University Press, 1988.

Shafaat Ahmad Khan, *John Marshall in India: Notes and Observations in Bengal (1668-1672,*. Oxford University Press, 1927.

R.C. Majumdar and A.D. Pusalker, eds. *The Vedic Age,*Vol.1, History and Culture of the Indian People, London: George Allen & Unwin Ltd, 1951.

James Prinsep, *Benares Illustrated* ed, O.P. Kejariwal, India: Vishwavidyalaya Prakashan, (1830) 1996.

———. 1832. *Benares, A Brahmin placing a garland on the holiest spot in the sacred city.* Lithograph. http://www.bl.uk/onlinegallery/onlineex/apac/other/019xzz000007512u00002000.html

Henry Thoby Prinsep, James Prinsep, *Essays on Indian Antiquities: Historic, Numismatic, and Palæographic,* United Kingdom: J. Murray, 1858.

The Quarterly Oriental Magazine, Review, and Register, India: Thacker and Company, 1825.

Mark Twain, *Following the Equator: A Journey Around the World. Hartford,* American Publishing Company, 1897.

Chapter 5: The Daniells

Mildred Archer, *Artist Adventures in Eighteenth Century India: Thomas and William Daniell,* United Kingdom: Spink, 1974.

———. *Early views of India: the picturesque journeys of Thomas and William Daniell, -1794: the complete aquatints,* New York, N.Y.: Thames and Hudson, 1980.

Louis de Grandpré, *A Voyage in the Indian Ocean and to Bengal, undertaken in the Years 1789 and 1790: Containing an Account of the Sechelles Islands and Trincomale,* London: G. and J. Robinson, 1803.

George Mitchell, *India Yesterday and Today: Two Hundred Years of Architectural and Topographical Heritage in India,* United Kingdom: Swan Hill Press, 1998.

Thomas Sutton, *The Daniells: Artists and Travellers,* United Kingdom: Bodley Head, 1954.

Masashi Suzuki and S.H. Clark, eds. *The Reception of Blake in the Orient,* United Kingdom: Bloomsbury Publishing, 2006.

Chapter 6: Henry Thomas Colebrooke

Asiatic Researches: Or, Transactions of the Society Instituted in Bengal, for Inquiring Into the History and Antiquities, the Arts, Sciences, and Literature, of Asia, United Kingdom: John Murray, 1818.

Charles Edward Buckland, *Dictionary of Indian Biography*, New York: Haskell House Publishers, 1968.

T.E. Colebrooke, *The Life of H. T. Colebrooke, by his son, Sir T. E. Colebrooke*, United Kingdom: Trübner & Company, 1873.

S. Ramaswami Iyengar, 'Henry T. Colebrooke', *Eminent Orientalists*, India: Cosmo Publications, 2000.

Journal of the Asiatic Society of Bengal, Vol. 6(2), Calcutta: The Baptist Mission Press, 1837.

O.P. Kejariwal, *The Asiatic Society of Bengal and the Discovery of India's Past, 1784-1838*, New York: Oxford University Press, 1988.

M. Moncalm, *The Origin of Thought and Speech*, United Kingdom: K. Paul, 1905. 22.

'Notices of the Life of Henry Thomas Colebrooke, Esq., by His Son', *The Journal of the Royal Asiatic Society of Great Britain and Ireland* 5(1):1–60, 1839. <http://www.jstor.org/stable/25181968>

Friedrich Max Müller, *Chips from a German Workshop: Essays chiefly on the science of language with index to vols 3 & 4*, United States: Scribner, Armstrong and Company, 1876.

Rosane Rocher and Ludo Rocher, *The Making of Western Indology: Henry Thomas Colebrooke and the East India Company*, United Kingdom: Taylor & Francis, 2014.

John Shore, *Memoirs of the Life, Writings and Correspondence, of Sir William Jones*, United Kingdom: Brettell, printer, 1806.

The Asiatic Journal and Monthly Register for British and Foreign India, China, and Australia, United Kingdom: Parbury, Allen, and Company, 1838.

Transactions of the Royal Asiatic Society of Great Britain and Ireland, Vol. 12, United Kingdom: Royal Asiatic Society, 1827.

Chapter 7: Horace Hayman Wilson

Frederick Charles Danvers, Percy Wigram, Monier Monier-Williams, Steuart Colvin Bayley, Brand Sapte, *Memorials of Old Haileybury College*, United Kingdom: A. Constable, 1894.

Shumboo Chunder Dey, 'Horace Hayman Wilson', *Eminent Orientalists*, India: Cosmo Publications, 2000.

Journal of the Royal Asiatic Society of Great Britain & Ireland, United Kingdom: Cambridge University Press for the Royal Asiatic Society, 1860.

Charles Knight, ed. *The English Cyclopædia: A New Dictionary of Universal Knowledge*, United Kingdom: Bradbury and Evans, 1858.

David Kopf, 'The Historiography of British Orientalism, 1772–1992', *Objects of Enquiry: The Life, Contributions, and Influence of Sir William Jones (1746-1794)*, eds. Garland Cannon and Kevin R. Brine, United Kingdom: NYU Press, 1995.

The Asiatic Journal and Monthly Register for British and Foreign India, China, and Australia, United Kingdom: Parbury, Allen, and Company, 1832.

'University Intelligence', *The Times*, 17 March 1832.

Chapter 8: Sir Monier Monier-Williams

Georgina Adelaïde Müller, ed. *The Life and Letters of the Right Honourable Friedrich Max Müller*, New York: Longmans, Green, 1902.

'Editorial', *The Times*, 29 October 1860.

'History of the Old Indian Institute', *Oxford Martin School*. Web. <https://www.oxfordmartin.ox.ac.uk/about/old-indian-institute/>.

Saral Jhingran, *Aspects of Hindu Morality*, India: Motilal Banarsidass Publishers, 1989.

Gerald Parsons and John Wolffe, eds. *Religion in Victorian Britain: Culture and empire*, UK: Manchester University Press, 1988.

'University Intelligence', *The Times*, 8 December 1860.

Monier Monier-Williams, *A Sanskrit-English Dictionary Etymologically and Philologically Arranged with special reference to Cognate Indo-European Languages*, Oxford University Press, 1899.

———. *Indian Wisdom; Or Examples of the Religious, Philosophical, and Ethical Doctrines of the Hindus: With a Brief History of the Chief Departments of Sanskrit Literature, and Some Account of the Past and Present Condition of India, Moral and Intellectual*, United Kingdom: Allen, 1876.

Chapter 9: Frederic Salmon Growse

Frederic Salmon Growse, *Bulandshahr: Or, Sketches of an Indian District: Social, Historical and Architectural*, India: Medical Hall Press, 1884.

———. *Mathurá: A District Memoir*, India: North-western Provinces and Oudh Government Press, 1874.

R.C. Prasad, ed. *The Rāmāyaṇa of Tulasīdāsa*, India: Motilal Banarsidass, 1987.

Chapter 10: Sir George Abraham Grierson

Mildred Archer, and William Archer, *India Served and Observed*, United Kingdom: BACSA, 1994.

George Abraham Grierson, *Bihār Peasant Life: Being a Discursive Catalogue of the Surroundings of the People of that Province: with Many Illustrations from Photographs Taken by the Author*, India: Bengal Secretariat Press, 1885.

———. *Linguistic Survey of India*, Vol. 1, India: Office of the Superintendent of Government Printing, India, 1927.

Gramophone Records of the Languages and Dialects of the Madras Presidency: Text of Passages, India: Commissioner of Museums, Government Museum, 1927.

R.L. Turner and F.W. Thomas, 'George Abraham Grierson', *Proceedings of the British Academy*, London: Oxford University Press, 1942.

Siddartha Sen, 'George Abraham Grierson, 1851-1941', Hermathena, no. 172: 39–55, 2002. http://www.jstor.org/stable/23041283.

R.L. Turner and H.W. Bailey, *Indian and Iranian Studies: Presented to George Abraham Grierson on His Eighty-fifth Birthday, 7th January, 1936*, United Kingdom: School of Oriental Studies, 1936.

Chapter 11: James Fergusson

Mildred Archer, R.W. Lightbown, *India Observed: India as Viewed by British Artists, 1760-1860: an Exhibition Organised by the Library of the Victoria and Albert Museum as Part of the Festival of India, 26 April-5 July 1982*, Netherlands: Victoria and Albert Museum, 1982.

Dictionary of National Biography, United Kingdom: Macmillan, 1889.

Robert Elwall, 'James 'Fergusson (1808 to 1886): A Pioneering Architectural Historian', *RSA Journal*, United Kingdom: Royal Society of Arts, 1990.

James Fergusson, *An Historical Inquiry Into the True Principles of Beauty in Art: More Especially with Reference to Architecture*, United Kingdom: Longman, Brown, Green, and Longmans, 1849.

———. *A History of Architecture in All Countries: From the Earliest Times to the Present Day*, United States: Dodd, Mead, 1885.

———. *History of Indian and Eastern Architecture*, United Kingdom: J. Murray, 1876.

M.S. Iyengar, 'James Fergusson', *Eminent Orientalists*, India: Cosmo Publications, 2000.

Peter Kohane, 'From Scotland to India: the Sources of James Fergusson's Theory of Architecture's "True Styles"', *ABE Journal. Architecture beyond Europe, no. 14–15 (July)*, 2019.

John Burton-Page, 'Mughal Architecture', *Indian Islamic Architecture: Forms and Typologies, Sites and Monuments*, ed. George Michell, 20:27–33. Brill, 2008.

'Sketch of James Fergusson', *The Popular Science Monthly*, United States: Popular Science Publishing Company, 1887.

Chapter 12: Brian Houghton Hodgson

Arthur Howell, *Education in British India, Prior to 1854, and in 1870-71*, India: Office of the Superintendent of Government Printing, 1872.

William Wilson Hunter, *Life of Brian Houghton Hodgson: British Resident at the Court of Nepal, Member of the Institute of France; Fellow of the Royal Society; a Vice-president of the Royal Asiatic Society, Etc*, United Kingdom: J. Murray, 1896.

The Spectator, Vol. 78, 6 March 1897, United Kingdom: F.C. Westley, 1897.

Chapter 13: Sir Alexander Cunningham

Alexander Cunningham, *Four Reports Made During the Years, 1862-63-64-65*, Vol. 1, India: Government Central Press, 1871.

Ancient India, India: Director General of Archaeology in India, 1953.

Archaeological Survey of India, Vol. 5, India: Government central Press, 1875.

Kurush Dalal, 'Alexander Cunningham: Digging Deep', *Live History India*, 4 January 2020. Web. <https://s3.ap-south-1.amazonaws.com/img.livehistoryindia.com/wp-content/uploads/2020/01/Alexander_Cunningham_of_the_ASI_02-scaled.jpg>

Lepel Griffin, *Famous Monuments of Central India*, United Kingdom: Autotype Company, 1886.

John Keay, *India Discovered: The Achievement of the British Raj*, Windward, 1981.

Journal of the Asiatic Society of Bombay, India: Asiatic Society of Bombay, 1969.

M.A. Sherring, *The Sacred City of the Hindus: An Account of Benares in Ancient and Modern Times*, United Kingdom: Trübner & Company, 1868.

Upinder Singh, *The Discovery of Ancient India: Early Archaeologists and the Beginnings of Archaeology*, India: Permanent Black, 2004.

'The Alexander We Forgot: Indian Archaeology Owes Much to Sir Cunningham', *Firstpost*. 22 February 2014. Web. <https://www.firstpost.com/india/the-alexander-we-forgot-indian-archaeology-owes-much-to-sir-cunningham-1403685.html>.

Chapter 14: Vincent Arthur Smith

'Editorial', *Statesman*, May 1958.

Nayanjot Lahiri, *Finding Forgotten Cities: How the Indus Civilization was Discovered*, India: Hachette India, 2012.

David Murphy, 'Smith, Vincent Arthur', *Dictionary of Irish Biography*, 2021. Web. <https://www.dib.ie/biography/smith-vincent-arthur-a8154>.

Vincent A. Smith, *Akbar the Great Mogul, 1542-1605*, Oxford: Clarendon Press, 1917.

———. *The Early History of India*, India: Atlantic Publishers & Distributors (P) Limited, 1999.

———. *The Settlement Officer's Manual for the North-Western Provinces*, India: North-Western Provinces and Oudh Government Press, 1881.

C.S. Srinivasachari, 'Vincent Smith', *Eminent Orientalists*, India: Cosmo Publications, 2000.

Romila Thapar, 'Ashoka - A Retrospective', *Economic and Political Weekly*, Vol. 44(55), 2009.

R. Vajreswari, *A Handbook for History Teachers*, India: Allied Publishers, 1966.

Chapter 15: Sir John Hubert Marshall

John Cumming, ed. *Revealing India's Past: A Record Of Archaeological Conservation And Exploration In India And Beyond*, Kiribati: India Society, 1939.

George Nathaniel Curzon, *Lord Curzon in India: Being a Selection from His Speeches as Viceroy & Governor-general of India 1898-1905*, United Kingdom: Macmillan and Company, limited, 1906.

G.N. Das, 'John Marshall 1876-1958', *American Anthropologist*, Vol. 61(6): 1071–74, 1959. http://www.jstor.org/stable/666782.

L.J.L. Dundas, *The Life of Lord Curzon: Being the Authorized Biography of George Nathaniel, Marquess Curzon of Kedleston, K.G.*, United Kingdom: Boni and Liveright, 1928.

India, *The Ancient Monuments Preservation Act*, 1904.

John Keay, *India Discovered: The Achievement of the British Raj*, Windward, 1981.

Nayanjot Lahiri, *Finding Forgotten Cities: How the Indus Civilization was Discovered*, India: Hachette India, 2012.

Walter Roper Lawrence, *The India We Served*, United Kingdom: Cassell and Company, 1928.

John Hubert Marshall, *A Guide to Sanchi*, India: Superintendent Government Printing, India, 1918.

———. *Taxila: An Illustrated Account of Archaeological Excavations Carried Out at Taxila Under the Orders of the Government of India Between the Years 1913 and 1934. Plates*, India: Motilal Banarsidass, 1951.

ACKNOWLEDGEMENTS

WE DECIDED TO WORK ON THIS BOOK AFTER A PERIOD OF sustained thought and a bit of research. Besides the assortment of books we have collected over the years, it also helped that Gautam's grandfather – Jogendranath Gupta, a well-known writer and historian of Bengal whose career spanned the first half of the twentieth century – had a sizeable collection of books in both Bengali and English relating to various aspects of India's history. What really kept us going was the enthusiasm of our daughter Tanya who would call us in the middle of the night from Washington DC to ensure that we were on the right track and not losing steam. We were also encouraged at every stage by Rupa's mother. We are indebted to Dr Siddharta Sen, Professor Emeritus of Trinity College, Dublin, who provided us with some little-known facts about Sir George Grierson. Last but not the least, we greatly appreciate the valuable assistance of the people at Hachette India, especially Poulomi Chatterjee and Swarnima Narayan, whose help has been crucial for the production of this book.